AUSTIN
Food Crawls
SECOND EDITION

AUSTIN
Food Crawls

SECOND EDITION

Kelsey Kennedy

TOURING *the* **NEIGHBORHOODS**
ONE BITE *&* **LIBATION** *at a* **TIME**

Globe Pequot

ESSEX, CONNECTICUT

Globe Pequot

An imprint of The Globe Pequot Publishing Group, Inc.
64 South Main Street
Essex, CT 06426
www.globepequot.com

Distributed by NATIONAL BOOK NETWORK

British Library Cataloguing in Publication Information available

Library of Congress Cataloging-in-Publication Data

Names: Kennedy, Kelsey (Food blogger), author.
Title: Austin food crawls : touring the neighborhoods one bite and libation at a time / Kelsey Kennedy.
Description: Second edition. | Essex, Connecticut : Globe Pequot, [2025] | Series: Food crawls | Includes index.
Identifiers: LCCN 2024027906 (print) | LCCN 2024027907 (ebook) | ISBN 9781493086818 (paperback) | ISBN 9781493086825 (epub)
Subjects: LCSH: Restaurants—Texas—Austin—Guidebooks. | Bars (Drinking establishments)—Texas—Austin—Guidebooks. | Food—Texas—Austin—Guidebooks. | Austin (Tex.)—Guidebooks.
Classification: LCC TX907.3.T42 A975 2025 (print) | LCC TX907.3.T42 (ebook) | DDC 647.9576431—dc23/eng/20240626
LC record available at https://lccn.loc.gov/2024027906
LC ebook record available at https://lccn.loc.gov/2024027907

Printed in India

Contents

Introduction

I SINCERELY HOPE YOU'RE HUNGRY.

(Like, *really* hungry.)

My job when writing this book was to divide Austin into neighborhoods and provide you, the reader, with a full day of eating through each neighborhood. The end result, which you're now holding, is over 100 restaurants, coffee shops, wine bars, breweries, food trucks, and bakeries in the greater Austin area.

And honestly, there are WAY more Austin restaurants that deserve to be in this book. I mean, I started with a list of nearly 300 restaurants that I absolutely adore and had to whittle it down to the 130+ that you see here now. (Honestly, it pains me a bit to even write that!)

Austin is a really cool city, and one of the problems with that is that there tend to be a handful of super popular restaurants that get ALL the attention among tourists, while there are a trillion fantastic restaurants that aren't getting the attention they deserve. I did my best to include both the new hotspots as well as some old tried-and-trues so that you can get a diverse sampling of the incredible culinary talent in this Texas city.

Of course, I couldn't cover *everything* in a single book. I hope you use *Austin Food Crawls* as a guide to get you going, but I know you'll discover your own local favorites while you're out and about. And if you're looking for more places to visit in Austin, come say hi to me at my blog, SoMuchLife.com. You can also find hundreds of Texas recommendations on my travel sites, TheAustinThings.com, TheSanAntonioThings.com, and TheWacoThings.com.

Ok, you ready? Let's eat.

Follow the Icons

 If you eat something outrageous and don't take a photo for Instagram, did you really eat it? These restaurants feature dishes that are Instagram famous. The foods must be seen (and snapped) to be believed, and luckily they taste as good as they look!

 Cheers to a fabulous night out in Austin! These spots add a little glam to your grub and are perfect for marking a special occasion.

 Follow this icon when you're crawling for cocktails. This symbol points out the establishments that are best known for their great drinks. The food never fails here, but be sure to come thirsty, too!

 This icon means that sweet treats are ahead. Bring your sweet tooth to these spots for dessert first (or second or third).

 Austin is for brunch. Look for this icon when crawling with a crew that needs sweet and savory (or an excuse to drink before noon).

THE DOWNTOWN AUSTIN CRAWL

1. Indulge in the best breakfast tacos in Austin at **VERACRUZ ALL NATURAL**, 111 E. CESAR CHAVEZ ST., AUSTIN, (512) 665-2713, VERACRUZ ALLNATURAL.COM

2. Enjoy an expertly prepared cappuccino at **HOUNDSTOOTH COFFEE**, 401 CONGRESS AVE. #100C, AUSTIN, (512) 394-6051, HOUNDSTOOTH COFFEE.COM

3. Linger over a gorgeous Mexican brunch at **LA CONDESA**, 400 W. 2ND ST., AUSTIN, (512) 499-0300, LACONDESA.COM

4. Stop by **WALTON'S FANCY AND STAPLE** FOR A LAZY WEEKDAY BREAKFAST, 609 W. 6TH ST., AUSTIN, (512) 542-3380, WALTONSFANCY ANDSTAPLE.COM

5. Find some comforting eats at **QI MODERN CHINESE RESTAURANT**, 835 W. 6TH ST. #114, AUSTIN, (512) 474-2777, QIAUSTIN.COM

6. Sneak in a pre-dinner martini at **SMALL VICTORY**, 108 E. 7TH ST., AUSTIN, SMALLVICTORY.BAR

7. Escape to Mexico City at **COMEDOR**, 501 COLORADO ST., AUSTIN, COMEDORTX.COM

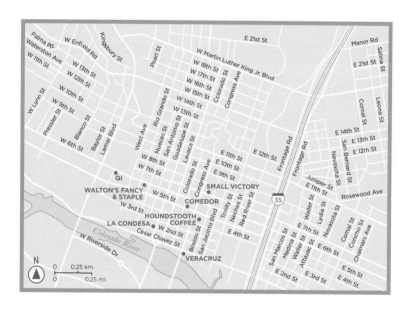

Downtown Austin

Where Austinites Live, Work, and Play

HOME OF THE STATE CAPITOL BUILDING, THE FAMOUS "BAT Bridge," and lots of places to eat and drink, Downtown Austin truly is the heart of our city. When Edwin Waller, the first mayor of Austin, was asked to construct a new town in the 1830s, he chose the 15 square blocks between Shoal and Waller Creek (east to west) and 15th Street and the Colorado River (north to south) that now make up the majority of downtown.

While you can still find historical landmarks, office buildings, and shopping districts, it's mostly massive residential towers that have been filling Austin in the last several years. As more people and big-name tech companies call downtown Austin home, the restaurant and bar scene has been consistently opening more options to accommodate the increasing foot traffic.

Downtown Austin can be broken into several districts for easy navigation:

2ND STREET DISTRICT: Get your retail therapy on! This is downtown Austin's largest shopping street.

HISTORIC 6TH STREET DISTRICT: Also known as "Dirty Sixth," this is Austin's go-to party street for live music and bars. You'll see a minimum of five bachelorette parties here on any given Saturday night!

SEAHOLM DISTRICT: Formerly home of the Seaholm Power Plant, this area has been renovated and is now a beautiful place to live, shop, and eat.

RED RIVER DISTRICT: Home to several of the city's hottest nightclubs including Stubb's, Barbarella, and Mohawk.

CONGRESS AVENUE: Originally the largest north-south street in Austin, running from Congress on the north and the Colorado River on the south. It's now a home to historic sites like the State Capitol and the Paramount Theater. (Congress was later extended south of the river; read about it in the South Congress Crawl!)

And of course, there's Rainey Street, which we'll cover in the next chapter. That street deserves its own day of eating!

1

INDULGE IN THE BEST BREAKFAST TACOS AT VERACRUZ ALL NATURAL

Ok, ok . . . let's just start with this: Claiming any breakfast taco as the "best in Austin" is a really bold statement. Flip to the back of the book to see the breakfast taco crawl, and you'll become pretty familiarized with the many fantastic breakfast tacos in this city. There are a lot of great ones to try!

But if you're in downtown Austin and you're looking for a great breakfast taco, stop by the walk-up window to **VERACRUZ ALL NATURAL**. Owners (and sisters!) Reyna and Maritza Vasquez grew up in Veracruz, Mexico. They learned all about using fresh, organic ingredients to cook delicious food. And in 2008 they opened their first trailer here in Austin. The massive amount of growth in their business is, quite frankly, because these tacos are so damn delicious.

The migas taco should definitely be on your order. It's full of scrambled eggs, pico de gallo, and crunchy tortilla chips, with cheese, cilantro, and avocado on top. And if you're looking for a delicious veggie-forward breakfast, try the Reyna taco. It's filled with a rainbow of delicately cooked veggies like mushrooms, carrots, red bell peppers, spinach, and onion.

Of course, you can't forget about their delicious fresh-pressed juices! Since Austin is hot, hot, hot for most of the year, the bright agua frescas,

smoothies, and fruit and veggie juices are a great way to kick-start your morning.

Pro-tip: This walk-up window of Veracruz All Natural is next to the Congress Avenue Bridge, which is where the famous Austin bat colony resides. If you're in Austin in the summer when the bats come out for their feeding, plan on stopping by Veracruz for some tacos, chips, and guacamole before finding your spot on the bat bridge to watch the show.

Next up: How about some coffee?

2 ENJOY AN EXPERTLY PREPARED CAPPUCCINO AT HOUNDSTOOTH COFFEE

Walk into **HOUNDSTOOTH,** and you're guaranteed an exceptional cup of coffee. But more than that, you're guaranteed an experience. At this point in your coffee journey, you probably recognize that drinking coffee is about more than just getting caffeinated in the morning. It's about connecting with humans, and Houndstooth has the friendliest baristas (and the best coffee program) in Austin.

Houndstooth was at the forefront of the specialty coffee movement in Austin. What started as a single cafe in Austin has now expanded across Texas, including several cafes that serve cocktails. This Congress Avenue location, in the iconic Frost Bank Tower and lovingly referred to as the "Frost" cafe, is an energizing place to start your morning before exploring the rest of downtown Austin. It's tucked into the corner of a high-rise office building, and there's a steady stream of people making their way in and out the door. Bright music plays on a speaker, and the bold red wall at the front stands out amid the otherwise neutral, calming tones of the cafe.

As you make a selection, a barista will gladly help you navigate through various roasts that are offered on the menu. This is especially great if

"The Pattern of Coffee and People." What does Houndstooth Coffee's motto mean, anyway?

"At Houndstooth we believe each interaction has the potential to be a memorable, venerable moment to be weaved in the Pattern of Coffee and People. We get 30 seconds to a minute each day with people, but over months and years, those moments develop into an intricate and beautiful pattern of taking care of our guests."
—Paul Henry, Houndstooth cofounder

you're new to coffee and need help exploring the subtle variations in mouthfeel and flavor profiles. And maybe you're not interested in "fancy" coffee and you just want a quick cup to wake you up? There's always the batch brew, kept fresh throughout the morning and easy to order.

While you're sipping your coffee and enjoying that first jolt of caffeine, enjoy a leisurely 8-minute walk to our next destination: brunch at La Condesa.

3

LINGER OVER A GORGEOUS MEXICAN BRUNCH AT LA CONDESA

The restaurant scene in downtown Austin is constantly turning over and creating new concepts, but the modern interior Mexican cuisine at **LA CONDESA** has remained a favorite among locals and visitors alike since 2009. La Condesa's weekend brunch is one of my favorites because this lively spot in the heart of downtown has the trifecta of a perfect dining experience: quality food, exceptional hospitality, and a beautiful ambience.

You'll walk in the stunning space and immediately notice a bright

ceiling-height mural on the restaurant's back wall. If you look closely, you'll see that it's La Condesa's way of paying homage to corn, which is at the forefront of nearly every brunch dish on the menu.

I love starting my brunch with their guacamole, which is topped with pico de gallo and served with a stack of crispy corn tostadas served in a cloth-covered basket. That, or the *queso flameado* (which is served with soft corn tortillas) paired with a pineapple-mint mimosa will get the good times rolling!

Have you ever had a churro waffle? It's just as delicious as it sounds. La Condesa prepares a soft, sweet waffle made of churro batter that's covered in cinnamon and sugar and topped with a slightly tangy Oaxacan crema and house-made grapefruit-hibiscus jam. And if you're looking for a place to get the best huevos rancheros in Austin, be sure to order them here. The restaurant's

house-made corn tostadas are crisp and flavorful, holding up nicely to the black beans, guajillo, avocado, and cotija.

Ok, let's say you're not free on the weekend but you still want a really good WEEKDAY brunch spot? The next stop is going to be perfect for you!

"Austin has experienced amazing growth for **decades**, and the favorite constant has been music and the arts. As those factors experience the spotlight, the food scene has taken over with a defined sense of purpose and delicious intent. Food in Austin, Texas is absolutely enjoying its glow up!"

– *Chef Rick Lopez, La Condesa*

4

STOP BY WALTON'S FANCY AND STAPLE FOR A LAZY WEEKDAY BREAKFAST

WALTON'S FANCY AND STAPLE is a restaurant, bakery, and gift shop in a historic 6th Street building. It has a nostalgic general-store feel with an elegant twist. The large overhead menu features breakfast staples like challah french toast, breakfast tacos, and shrimp and poblano-cheddar Gouda grits. The cold sandwiches, pressed panini, soups, and salads provide a vast assortment of tasty lunch options.

Right when you walk in, the glass cases near the entrance will tempt you with all sorts of colorful sweets and treats, like salty oat cookies, cream cheese brownies, and Walton's famous Honey-Bee Cake, a honey-almond cake layered with caramel buttercream and topped with ganache. Don't miss out on the Golden Eggs, which are nutmeg-infused yellow cakes dipped in melted butter and coated in cinnamon and sugar.

Whether you're stopping for a full meal or just a little bite to take on the road, this is a great place to pick up a scrumptious treat, unique souvenir, or a bouquet of flowers for a friend.

We've talked a lot about eats and drinks for your morning, so let's move on to an excellent lunch spot in downtown Austin.

5 FIND SOME COMFORTING EATS AT QI MODERN CHINESE RESTAURANT

QI is an absolutely gorgeous downtown Austin restaurant that serves modern Chinese cuisine. While they are very popular for their weekend dim sum brunch, my favorite time to visit is for a delicious weekday lunch.

Chef Ling Qi Wu realized that healthy, nourishing food could easily be at the forefront of her restaurants if she focused on quality, organic ingredients, sourced as locally as possible. So the menu is packed full of bright veggies, fresh herbs, and humanely treated meat that's all prepared with love and care.

What to order? The Shanghai Soup Dumplings to start! All of Chef Ling's restaurants (she has quite the growing empire here in Austin) feature these small, delicate dumplings that

are served in a basket and bursting with a rich, savory broth and minced meat. The pot stickers, egg rolls, and fried beef *bao* are excellent options if you're dining with a crowd. This is a great place to order a bunch of starters to share with the table.

The lunch entrees are served with your choice of soup and steamed rice. And while they might look familiar (sesame chicken, salt and pepper shrimp, beef with peppers), go ahead and raise your expectations right now. The Chinese entrees you'll eat at Qi are the elevated, healthier, holy-wow-this-is-delicious versions of the classic dishes you might have tried somewhere else.

Before we move on to dinner, I'm going to share the best spot in downtown Austin for a pre-dinner martini.

6 SNEAK IN A PRE-DINNER MARTINI AT SMALL VICTORY

The first time I went to **SMALL VICTORY**, I walked right past it before realizing I had arrived. The sign on the door is small, and the windowless second-story bar is invisible from the street, but these expertly prepared cocktails have become an Austin favorite for pre- or post-dinner drinks.

Owners Josh Loving and Brian Stubbs have worked in some of the most impressive cocktail bars in Austin, and they know that a dark and sultry speakeasy atmosphere is cool, but the backbone of a great cocktail bar has to come from great drinks. Their progressive ice program means that all of the ice is made in-house. The result? Your drink will be prepared as cold as possible, without being watered down by ice that melts too quickly.

Small Victory undoubtedly has the best martini program in Austin. Whether you're a total pro at placing your martini order or you're a martini newbie, the menu makes it easy. It's illustrated as a flowchart to walk you through your choices (gin or vodka; degree of dryness; twist, olive, or onion?) so you can place an order in full confidence.

The popular mixed drinks are offered as a title and a list of ingredients, so ask your bartender for suggestions if you're unsure what to get. Although I'm not typically one to go for tiki drinks, Small Victory's Hurricane is scrumptious. It's made with Jamaican rum and house-made passion fruit syrup. It's classy, a little sassy, and won't make you feel like the odd one out if you want a sweet drink while everyone else is sipping gin martinis.

If you need some nourishment to go with your booze, small plates of Antonelli's cheese, charcuterie, olives, and nuts are available. Save some room for dinner, though; there are plenty of award-winning dinner restaurants in downtown Austin, and Comedor is at the top of the list.

7 ESCAPE TO MEXICO CITY AT COMEDOR

COMEDOR is one of the most beautiful restaurants in downtown Austin, but you might not expect that from the exterior. With its almost speakeasy-inspired architecture, this upscale Mexican restaurant is a plain black brick one-story building on the corner of Colorado and 5th Street. But once you walk in, you'll notice that some of those black bricks are actually light-emitting, resulting in a soft hue of natural sunlight. That glow, paired with the giant windows near the top of the soaring ceilings, pulls in a flood of brightness that fills the restaurant.

The cuisine at Comedor is just as impressive as the architecture. The style is "modern Mexican," which is a bit hard to pin down, because the word modern in front of any cuisine means it's mostly up to the

chef's interpretation. But you can expect plenty of corn (soft tortillas and crunchy tostadas), seafood (zingy crudo, mussels in red chorizo and XO sauce), and a few larger plates of grilled meat.

The one thing on Comedor's menu that doesn't ever change? The bone marrow tacos. They're a must-order item. Your server will provide a basket of warm tortillas and a few giant pieces of roasted bone marrow on a bed of greens. You'll tip the bone over the tortilla and let the melty, decadent marrow slide on to the tortilla. There's plenty of acidity added to the dish to balance out the richness, and you can fill the tortilla with some of the greens to add volume. It's one of the most unique taco experiences in the city of Austin.

Other than the bone marrow tacos, the menu at Comedor will most likely rotate. Plan on ordering about 3-5 plates of both small and large dishes for a party of two people.

THE RAINEY STREET CRAWL

1. Start your weekend with a live jazz brunch at **GERALDINE'S**, 605 DAVIS ST., AUSTIN, (512) 476-4755, HOTELVANZANDT.COM/GERALDINES

2. Take on the largest tap wall in Austin at **BANGER'S SAUSAGE HOUSE AND BEER GARDEN**, 79 RAINEY ST., AUSTIN, (512) 432-5533, BANGERSAUSTIN.COM

3. Satisfy all your taco cravings at **ASADOR**, 88½ RAINEY ST., AUSTIN, ASADORTACOS.COM

4. Sip on Rainey's best cocktails at **HALF STEP**, 75½ RAINEY ST., AUSTIN, (512) 391-1877, HALFSTEPBAR.COM

5. Taste bites of farm-to-table fare at **EMMER & RYE**, 51 RAINEY ST. #110, AUSTIN, (512) 366-5530, EMMERANDRYE.COM

6. Nosh on pizza and sip well drinks at **LUSTRE PEARL**, 94 RAINEY ST., AUSTIN, DUNLAPATX.COM/LUSTRE-PEARL-RAINEY

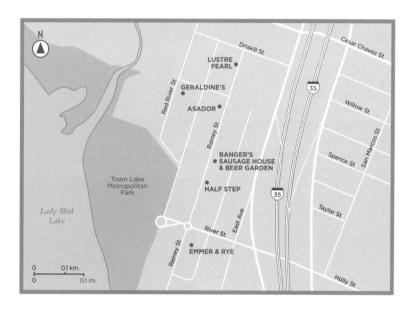

Rainey Street

Austin's Nightlife Street

ALTHOUGH IT IS TECHNICALLY A PART OF DOWNTOWN AUSTIN, Rainey Street has earned its own chapter in this book because it's THE go-to party street of bars, restaurants, and food trucks in Austin. Anyone who's visiting Austin wants to know, "where should I eat and drink on Rainey Street?"

Tucked away on (what used to be) a sleepy residential street, Rainey Street was gradually transformed into Austin's hottest nightlife scene. The small, one-story bungalows that quietly lined Rainey Street were excellent candidates to be renovated into quirky bars. Each one was built with its own theme, many of them with darling front patios and huge backyard spaces for yard games or intimate concerts during the South by Southwest (SXSW) Festival.

Of course, as Rainey's popularity grew, big-name investors started coming in, wiping out the bungalow bars, and building high-rise condos and hotels in their place. What are we left with? A mix of modern high-rises and historic bungalow bars for the ultimate night out in Austin, Texas.

Here's the secret to Rainey Street: While there are plenty of folks who simply want to spend the night out on Rainey to get completely trashed, there are actually a handful of exceptional spots to eat, drink, and listen to music. I've scoped them out for you so you can have a game plan for this iconic street in downtown Austin.

1

START YOUR WEEKEND WITH A
LIVE JAZZ BRUNCH AT GERALDINE'S

Named after a beloved guinea fowl that used to roam Rainey Street, **GERALDINE'S** is a music-inspired restaurant tucked away in the fourth floor of the Hotel Van Zandt. Step off the elevator and you'll be swept away to a unique Austin music venue.

The restaurant offers live music 7 days a week, and one of their most popular meals is the weekend jazz brunch. Here, you can enjoy anything from local musicians to national bands, all performing on an intimate stage.

While you're enjoying the music, order from the Texas-inspired menu of classic brunch fare. The buttermilk biscuits with maple

honey butter are light and fluffy and the perfect shareable starter. For a bit of a Tex-Mex entree, try the chilaquiles topped with sunny-side-up eggs. The menu is also brimming with signature brunch cocktails to kick off your Rainey Street food crawl with some fun!

One of my favorite parts about Geraldine's is that it's adjacent to the Hotel Van Zandt rooftop pool. If you're lucky enough to be staying at this Rainey Street hotel, you could mosey over to the pool deck after your brunch and enjoy a few hours by the pool.

After brunch, let's keep the good times rolling by visiting the largest tap wall in Austin!

2

TAKE ON THE LARGEST TAP WALL IN AUSTIN AT BANGER'S SAUSAGE HOUSE AND BEER GARDEN

Bar-hopping on Rainey Street with a crowd? **BANGER'S** is your place. All of the seating is made up of long rows of picnic tables, making this an easy bet for your hungry party of 10.

As the name suggests, the restaurant mostly serves sausage and beer. All 30 varieties of sausage are made in-house, and the tap list is in the triple digits.

The sausage menu starts with the most basic offerings for those who want something familiar: bratwurst, kielbasa, and chicken apple. The Italian sausage and peppers is a flavorful meal with its hefty serving of bell peppers and onions cooked al dente, topped with aromatic cracked black pepper and torn basil.

Keep reading down the menu, and the sausage names get more and more eclectic. (Just one more restaurant doing its part to "Keep Austin Weird," folks!) Try the duck, bacon, and fig sausage for a sweet/savory combo, or the Salsa Very Verde if you can handle a bit of a spicy kick. Of course, there's also the smokehouse menu, which features all sorts of slow-smoked entrees like a pork shoulder sandwich, sweet and spicy pit ribs, and a hefty 1-pound wild boar sausage coil.

Like many Rainey Street bars, this one has a stage set up in the backyard. On any given weekend evening, live music fills the air and beer and good times are flowing. I'll cheers to that.

Watch out, because the next Rainey stop might ruin every other taco experience in your life. . . .

3 SATISFY ALL YOUR TACO CRAVINGS AT ASADOR

ASADOR's menu is small yet mighty, with just a few tacos that are made with creative fillings tucked inside delicious, soft flour tortillas that are a bit charred on the outside. The result? A mind-blowing variety of textures and flavors. Pair that with a cold agua fresca on a hot Austin evening, and you're ready for the ultimate meal from a walk-up window on Rainey Street.

The menu offers some specials (order those if they're available), but it typically has 5 options: brisket, carnitas, chicken pastor, vegetarian cauliflower, and a quesadilla. The vegetarian taco is smothered with a homemade Mexican mole, which is hella spicy. Watch out! In general, these tacos are pretty large and filling,

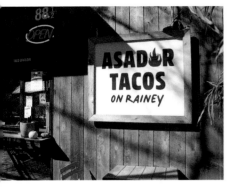

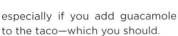

especially if you add guacamole to the taco—which you should.

Round out your order with some chips and a trio of dips, a beverage, and you'll be ready for wherever your food crawl leads you next. Which, if you're following this book as a guideline, will be one of the best cocktail spots on Rainey Street.

SIP ON RAINEY'S BEST COCKTAILS AT HALF STEP

You can order an average (overpriced) drink at almost any bar on Rainey, but if you're looking for an exceptional craft cocktail, one bar stands far above the rest: **HALF STEP**. *Esquire* magazine called this one of the best bars in the country.

What makes these cocktails so exceptional? Half Step gives special attention to an often-overlooked component of the cocktail: ice. Half Step is one of the few bars in Texas that makes its ice completely in-house, from start to finish. They start with an extensive filtration process, then freeze the water into massive, 350-pound blocks of clear ice. Using a modified band saw, they cut the ice into five custom shapes to be used for various cocktails. When you walk into the bar, you're ordering a cocktail that is not only made with homemade juices and syrups, but also homegrown ice.

The draft cocktails are an easy place to start. The Ginger Paloma, made with tequila, ginger, lime, grapefruit, and Mexican grapefruit soda, is refreshing on a warm Austin evening. If you choose to stray from the menu, have a chat with your bartender. Discuss your favorite cocktail ingredients,

pick a spirit, and watch your custom-made cocktail appear in front of you. (Just don't ask for something custom during peak hours. This place gets packed on the weekends!)

Now that you've imbibed award-winning cocktails, it's time to dine at an award-winning restaurant.

5

TASTE BITES OF FARM-TO-TABLE FARE AT EMMER & RYE

EMMER & RYE opened in 2015 and was immediately named one of Austin's Best New Restaurants by *Bon Appétit*. They've remained one of the best upscale restaurants in Austin due to their (borderline excessive?) obsession with sourcing hyper-locally, introducing new flavor profiles, and serving their guests the best farm-to-table cuisine possible. As the name suggests, the focus at **EMMER & RYE** is on the house-milled heirloom grains. This means that not only is the pasta homemade, but the flour to make the pasta is also milled right there in the restaurant. In addition to heirloom grains, Emmer & Rye is known for their in-house fermentation program, minimal waste, and seasonal menus.

Yes, the menu rotates with the seasons, but one menu item never gets cut: the Blue Beard Durum *cacio e pepe*. *Cacio e pepe* is a simple dish of pasta, cheese, and black pepper, but Emmer & Rye puts so much detail into preparing their chewy pasta and rich, creamy cheese, just order it and you'll see why this dish is a customer favorite. After my first bite, I made it a goal to order *cacio e pepe* around the country, trying to find one that matches the same quality of texture and flavor that Emmer & Rye can produce in their dish; I've had no luck thus far.

The ambience is inspired by restaurants in Copenhagen, where chef Kevin Fink spent time training. The Scandinavian-inspired design feels light and airy, with white tile walls, floor-to-ceiling windows, and a few pops of color from hanging plants and warm wood accents. There's a simplicity to the restaurant's design, which leaves space for the remarkable food to shine.

The night doesn't have to end here! Walk down the street to experience the best OG bar on Rainey Street.

6

NOSH ON PIZZA AND SIP WELL DRINKS AT LUSTRE PEARL

LUSTRE PEARL was the first bar on Rainey Street. People who were in Austin more than a decade ago know that this is the bar that actually made Rainey Street what it is today, which is a place to go for nightlife.

Here's where it might get a bit confusing: Lustre Pearl, which used to be at 97 Rainey Street, was forced to close to make room for a new high-rise development. But Bridget Dunlap, the person who created the bar, managed to save that historic 1895 bungalow, move it to east Austin, and open a "Lustre Pearl East" bar over there. You can visit that one, too! A few years later, Lustre Pearl reopened on Rainey Street, but this time in a different bungalow with a new address: 94 Rainey Street. We still like to think of her as the same old

OG bar, because the vibe is the same, and we love tradition.

The simple drink menu features a few signature cocktails, which are mostly light and refreshing and made to be enjoyed in hot Austin, Texas. The draft list includes a few local favorites from some of our craft breweries, as well as cans of domestic beer. If you love a good deal, stop by earlier in the day to take advantage of their happy hour for a few bucks off your drink order.

And if you need some carbs to soak up the booze, there's no better place to order a hot, delicious pizza than Via 313, the food truck parked in front of Lustre Pearl. This Detroit-style pizza is a rectangular pie that's made with a deep, fluffy crust, crispy on the edges and soft and light in the middle. It's topped with cheese and toppings first and then a few stripes of hearty tomato sauce on top. Try The Detroiter pizza, which is made with two different types of pepperoni.

The perfect night on Rainey Street ends with an Austin craft beer in one hand, a warm slice of deep-dish in the other, and some good local tunes played on a nearby stage. I'll cheers to that.

YOU'RE VISITING A US HISTORIC DISTRICT!

The Rainey Street Historic District includes 120 acres.

The street was added to the National Register of Historic Places in 1985.

Most of the homes on Rainey Street are bungalow-style, which is just the right size to be renovated into stylish bars!

While the street is a historic district, none of the individual buildings are designated as historic structures. That's why they keep getting torn down to make room for high-rises. Who knows what Rainey will look like in 10 years?

THE SOUTH CONGRESS CRAWL

1. Brunch in style at **CAFE NO SÉ**, 1603 S. CONGRESS AVE., AUSTIN, (512) 942-2061, CAFENOSEAUSTIN.COM

2. Chow down on an authentic New York–style pie at **HOME SLICE PIZZA**, 1415 S. CONGRESS AVE., AUSTIN, (512) 444-7437, HOMESLICEPIZZA.COM

3. Experience the famous flagship location of **TORCHY'S TACOS**, 1822 S. CONGRESS AVE., AUSTIN, (512) 916-9025, TORCHYSTACOS.COM

4. Grab your friends and indulge in fries and rosé at **JUNE'S ALL DAY**, 1722 S. CONGRESS AVE., AUSTIN, (512) 416-1722, JUNESALLDAY.COM

5. Enjoy a breezy afternoon at **SUMMER HOUSE ON MUSIC LANE**, 1101 MUSIC LN., AUSTIN, (512) 442-5341, WWW.BUNKHOUSEHOTELS.COM /SUMMER-HOUSE-ON-MUSIC-LANE

6. Snack on Tokyo-inspired street food at **LUCKY ROBOT**, 1303 S. CONGRESS AVE., (512) 444-8081, LUCKYROBOTRESTAURANT.COM

7. Make your inner-child happy with a double (or triple) scoop at **AMY'S ICE CREAMS**, 1301 S. CONGRESS AVE., (512) 440-7488, AMYSICECREAMS.COM

8. Dress up for date night at **PERLA'S**, the finest seafood restaurant in Austin, 1400 S. CONGRESS AVE., AUSTIN, (512) 291-7300, PERLAS AUSTIN.COM

9. Discover **WATERTRADE**, the coolest Japanese whisky bar in town, 1603 S. CONGRESS AVE., AUSTIN, (512) 994-0428, HTTPS://OTOKOAUSTIN .COM/WATERTRADE

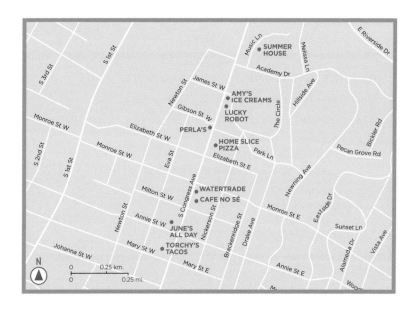

South Congress

Not Such a Tourist Trap

SOUTH CONGRESS AVENUE IS AUSTIN'S BIGGEST SHOPPING, entertainment, and tourist street, and it has a rich history. It was first paved with concrete in 1910 when a new bridge was built and streetcar lines were extended across the river, and since then it has continued to grow and evolve into what it is today. The Ann W. Richards Congress Avenue Bridge, which stretches across Lady Bird Lake, is sometimes called the "bat bridge" because it's home to the largest urban bat colony in the world. This bridge connects South Congress Avenue to downtown Austin.

South Congress is a good central "home base" for Austin visitors, with easy access to other parts of town and enough great restaurants to fill up a solid weekend of eating. This street is packed with boutique hotels, famous murals, iconic music venues, and a bunch of great places to go shopping at both national brand stores and local souvenir shops. I never get tired of wandering up and down the streets of SoCo on a busy Saturday morning, shopping and eating to my heart's content. Even though it's a trendy tourist area, South Congress has some of Austin's best restaurants where locals love hanging out. It's a brunch lover's paradise with multiple options (I'll mention a few of them in this chapter), lots of happy hour hotspots, and some fine-dining establishments that are perfect for wrapping up your day of shopping.

1

BRUNCH IN STYLE AT CAFE NO SÉ

CAFE NO SÉ is a bright corner spot nestled into the bottom floor of the South Congress Hotel, where you're likely to find well-dressed individuals gathering for breakfast before starting their days. Nearly everything here (even the floor) is photo-worthy, making this the perfect place for those of us who love taking pictures of our food. A communal table in the middle of the room can seat a large group, and smaller tables are scattered around the indoor space and outdoor patio for quiet brunchgoers who are looking for a fresh, seasonal menu on SoCo.

The pastries from James Beard Foundation Award semifinalist Amanda Rockman are worth the indulgence; I love sharing them with the table so I'm still hungry for a brunch entree. The *kouign amann* is a must-try item: It's a flaky pastry with layers of butter and sugar and a chewy, caramelized exterior.

Healthy brunch options include avocado toast, which looks stunning with crème fraîche, arugula, and Aleppo carrots heaped on top, or a hearty

savory quinoa bowl dressed in almond pesto with crispy little chickpeas sprinkled throughout. If you're on vacation and simply want to indulge, the buttermilk hotcakes are tall, fluffy pieces of heaven.

Not all of us are early morning risers, but thankfully Cafe No Sé offers an all-day menu that extends late into the evening. Fuel up for a fun day of exploring SoCo!

2 CHOW DOWN ON AN AUTHENTIC NEW YORK–STYLE PIE AT HOME SLICE PIZZA

These homemade, thin-crust, hand-tossed pies have won the hearts of locals and visitors alike, as is apparent by the crowd lined up on the sidewalk, waiting for a table inside **HOME SLICE PIZZA.**

Home Slice became a south Austin favorite immediately after it opened in the early 2000s because of its catchy name, friendly service, and (of course), delicious pies. The pizza became so popular, in fact, that the team at Home Slice bought the space next door and opened "More Home Slice," a walk-up counter for pizza by the slice that can be enjoyed on the small sidewalk patio. They also have a north Austin location with a playground for kids.

The menu, as with any traditional pizzeria, is fairly easy to navigate: The garlic knots with marinara and a big family-style salad are a great start to the meal. The thin, chewy-crust pizzas can be personalized with your own favorite toppings or enjoyed from the "tried and true" menu that Home Slice provides;

these are classics like pepperoni and mushroom, white clam pizza, and eggplant pie. The sub sandwiches are the most overlooked menu items, and every Austin local will tell you the same thing. The hot meatball sub is a soft and warm home-baked Italian roll filled with rich marinara sauce and oozy provolone, mozzarella, and Parmesan cheese and homemade meatballs. And I am slightly ashamed to admit that I was a regular customer here for five years before ever ordering the Italian sub. One bite of that fresh and chewy homemade bread full of a generous pile of Italian meat and cheese, and the cravings haven't stopped.

Because the pies at Home Slice Pizza are all cooked to order directly on a 2-inch stone, you'll have a little bit of time between placing your order and tasting your first bite of hot New York–style pizza; enjoy those garlic knots for starters, and your patience will be well rewarded.

Stroll down the street for another iconic Austin eatery.

TIP

THERE ARE LOTS OF FAMOUS MURALS ON SOUTH CONGRESS AVENUE.

Try to take a picture by these three:

"I Love You So Much," on the side of Jo's Coffee, 1300 S. Congress Ave.

"Willie For President," on the side of STAG, 100 E. Elizabeth St.

"Love From Austin," on the side of Prima Dora, 1912 S. Congress Ave.

3

EXPERIENCE THE FAMOUS FLAGSHIP LOCATION OF TORCHY'S TACOS

TORCHY'S TACOS is hardly considered an "Austin restaurant" anymore due to its rapid national expansion, but the truth is that Torchy's started right here in ATX. And if you're going to choose just one location in Austin to try that famous Torchy's queso and a fried avocado taco, head to the flagship restaurant on South Congress. The building was designed to mimic iconic drive-in diners from the 50s with bold red "X" beams and a bright "TORCHY'S" marquee across the top of the building. On busy weekends, like in March during SXSW, the line can extend out the front door, but the dining room and large pet-friendly patio provide plenty of seating.

Torchy's serves the whole menu all day, so you can order guacamole and chips at 7 a.m., or a Wrangler breakfast taco (scrambled eggs and potatoes with smoked beef brisket, jack cheese, and tomatillo sauce) at 10 p.m. These bold, creative tacos don't fit into the category of traditional Mexican tacos. Torchy's has their own taco culture! Feeling crazy? Try the Independent, a flour tortilla full of battered and fried portobello mushroom strips, refried black beans, avocado, and ancho aioli. Feeling a little bit tame? The beef or chicken fajita taco is always available for folks who don't want anything too spicy or wild.

Regardless of the taco you order, the green chile queso topped with fresh guacamole, cotija cheese, cilantro, and Torchy's spicy diablo sauce is always the right choice. It's widely regarded as Austin's favorite queso, and it's instantly addicting. Upgrade it to Hillbilly Queso and they'll add a scoop of Texas chorizo on top.

Tacos are great at all hours of the day, but what's the beverage equivalent? Our next stop has #RoséAllDay!

4

GRAB YOUR FRIENDS AND INDULGE IN FRIES AND ROSÉ AT JUNE'S ALL DAY

JUNE'S ALL DAY, which opened in 2016 and was immediately on Food & Wine's Best New Restaurants list, is an adorable corner cafe that offers an all-day bistro menu. I love stopping by in the morning to enjoy a lazy cup of coffee and a croissant on the small outdoor patio, or making dinner reservations for a Sunday night double date with my husband and two of our friends. June's is easy and comfortable.

The afternoon is a beautiful time to stop by, perch at the counter, and order a rosy pink burger with shoestring fries and a bottle of wine. The black-and-white tiles on the floor convey a classic, timeless elegance, and

the marble countertops mean that every photo you take of the food will be Insta-worthy.

If happy hour isn't your thing, the "all day" in the title means that you can stop in at all hours of the day to indulge. Breakfast and brunch are served daily with lovely items like a Farm Egg Omelet with Boursin, salted radish, and green salad, or a beautiful croque madame that will make you feel like you're in a French cafe. The menu extends from lunch into the late hours of the night with delectable entrees. Try the popular bone marrow Bolognese, a cozy dish with handkerchief pasta, kale, and salty parm, or the matzo ball caldo, a comforting soup made with poached chicken, veggies, and jalapeños.

June's is a charming oasis of calm amid the bustle on SoCo. Step inside to escape the Austin heat, set your shopping bags down for a rest, and ask your server what the sommelier has recently put on the wine menu. Cheers to the good life!

I'm going to offer one more recommendation for an afternoon rest stop, but this time it's waaaay on the other end of South Congress.

5

ENJOY A BREEZY AFTERNOON AT SUMMER HOUSE ON MUSIC LANE

There aren't many places on South Congress that feel quiet and secluded, but **SUMMER HOUSE** is one of them. This hotel restaurant on the ground floor of Hotel Magdelena is within the Music Lane district of South Congress. And while the shops and restaurants that are directly on SoCo are subject to all the foot traffic and noise that comes with that location, Summer House is tucked away and designed to feel, well, like a lazy, breezy lake house in the summer.

Being a hotel restaurant, **SUMMER HOUSE** offers their garden-fresh menu at almost any hour of the day for breakfast, lunch, happy hour, or dinner. My favorite time to stop by is in the late afternoon for a calm and casual happy hour. Small plates include fresh and crunchy crudités served with a bowl of hummus, caramelized onion dip with potato crisps, and their delectable smash burger, served with hand-cut fries and aioli. The bright cocktails are made with fresh herbs, local liquors, and often feature a splash of soda or sparkling wine to keep things light and refreshing.

Of course, the dinner menu is well worth perusing, if you choose to dine here for a full meal. I describe the menu to my friends as "a sophisticated take on casual food." It's the type of food you'd want to enjoy after being out on the lake all day, and you're ready for a plate of chicken with charred sweet potatoes and cashew habañero aioli, or a flaky, slightly sweet oak-grilled branzino with zingy green herb salsa and soft corn tortillas.

Summer House's patio is shaded and overlooks their courtyard garden. It truly is a hidden oasis on the bustling street of South Congress, and the perfect place to rest before turning in for the night.

Or, if you're feeling recharged and up for more fun, head back out to SoCo for another great spot for Austin eats.

6

SNACK ON TOKYO-INSPIRED STREET FOOD AT LUCKY ROBOT

Bright lights, fun neon colors, fish that has been imported from renowned Tsukiji Fish Market in Tokyo, and farm-to-table produce: **LUCKY ROBOT** brings Tokyo street food to the heart of Austin.

Sit on indoor swings (yes, swings) and order hot or cool apps, bowls, sushi and sashimi, maki rolls, and a beautiful selection from the daily market fish, flown in from Japan and around the world.

Sustainability is an important component to Lucky Robot's menu. They recognize that resources are limited, and humanity hasn't done the best job at treating our oceans with respect. Lucky Robot does their part to source sustainably. They were recently recognized by the James Beard Foundation Smart Catch Program as a leader in protecting the future of our oceans.

Lucky for you, there are many types of delectable (and safe!) fish to enjoy on the menu. The Chiki Toro is a signature nigiri made with Hawaiian bigeye tuna and house-cured lardo. It mimics the deep flavor of otoro (or "fatty tuna") with a sustainable version.

Try the hand-pressed pork and ginger dumplings with salsa macha and black vinegar, or an omakase chef's tasting if you want to try a little bit of everything on the menu.

Lucky Robot is next to Amy's Ice Creams. I try to save just a little bit of room so that I can head there for a scoop after dinner.

LUCKY ROBOT HAS A LOT OF SAKE ON THEIR MENU. NEW TO SAKE? HERE'S AN INTRODUCTION!

Nama sake is growing in popularity. *Nama* is unpasteurized and contains active enzymes that give a wonderful youthful, lively taste!

Sake is a source of umami, a natural flavor enhancer, also found in Parmesan, mushrooms, and tomatoes.

Tasting notes for sake range from butter to bananas Foster, from fresh mushroom to ripe cantaloupe.

There's a misconception that only cheap sake should be served warm. Warmed sake expresses aromas, tastes, and textures that are suppressed when served chilled.

The yeast used in sake production has an incredible impact on the aroma of sake. Yeast #9 is one of the most commonly used for highly aromatic *ginjo* and *daiginjo* sakes.

MAKE YOUR INNER CHILD HAPPY WITH A DOUBLE (OR TRIPLE) SCOOP AT AMY'S ICE CREAMS

I can tell you from experience that ice cream is a great way to endure the blistering Texas summers. Two or three scoops of ice cream, piled high and melting off a sweet vanilla waffle cone, have helped me make my way through decades of triple-digit summer temperatures. And if you're on SoCo and need a cool treat, **AMY'S ICE CREAMS** is your best bet.

Amy's has been Austin's most popular ice cream shop since 1984. There are locations all over town, but the South Congress walk-up window is still my favorite. It's just a few blocks away from the Ann W. Richards Congress Avenue Bridge (aka the "bat bridge"), where rows of people line up to watch the Mexican free-tailed bats emerge from their hiding place under the bridge every night from March to October. When I have guests in town, one of my favorite summer activities is to grab a scoop at Amy's (I love ordering Mexican vanilla with cookie dough and rainbow sprinkles) and walk a few blocks north to watch the bats.

Amy's has more than 350 rotating flavors . . . think you can try them all? Several flavors are always on the menu, like Mexican vanilla, sweet cream, and dark chocolate. The crazier flavors come and go, so I try to taste them while they're around; I love the spicy chipotle chocolate mixed with salted whiskey caramel, and Zilker mint chip. Once you eventually choose a flavor, you also have the option of adding crush'ns and toppings like pecans, oatmeal cookies, or marshmallows for thousands of flavor combinations.

After a long day of browsing the shops of South Congress, you'll be ready to unwind and savor a slow dinner at our next stop: Perla's.

8

DRESS UP FOR DATE NIGHT AT PERLA'S, THE FINEST SEAFOOD RESTAURANT IN AUSTIN

I can't think of a better way to finish up a day on SoCo than with a glorious evening spent at **PERLA'S**. This seafood restaurant is the epitome of what Austin, Texas, considers an "upscale" restaurant, which is to say . . . it's still very casual. The Gulf Coast–inspired seafood dishes are exceptional, the raw bar is among the best in the city, and the attentive staff is friendly and knowledgeable. But this is still Austin, Texas, and we love to wear jeans and sundresses and sandals. The MML Hospitality group (which also runs June's, listed earlier in this chapter!) has managed to create a special occasion restaurant that's still casual enough for Austin.

Perhaps it's because of the bright, twinkly lights on the patio,

the crisp, white tablecloths, or the icy trays of raw oysters being scurried around the room, but there's a definite spirit of elegance and celebration in the air.

Although fresh fish and oysters are flown in daily from both East and West Coasts, Gulf Coast seafood is emphasized. Start with the corn-meal-fried oysters with Chili Morita and slaw for the table, and try the crispy Texas Gulf snapper for a true taste of Texas's best seafood.

The oak-shaded outdoor patio, which faces South Congress Avenue, absorbs the energy from the lively tourist street. I think fondly of many happy evenings I've spent sipping coastal cocktails on Perla's giant patio with family and close friends.

9

DISCOVER WATERTRADE, THE COOLEST JAPANESE WHISKY BAR IN TOWN

There are a number of places in Austin that call themselves "speakeasy-style bars" and then loudly proclaim on their website, social media, and advertising, "WE'RE A SPEAKEASY!!" Hmm . . . is it still true at that point? **WATERTRADE**, a Japanese whisky bar on the second floor of the South Congress Hotel, is only accessible via a courtyard door at the top of 12 unmarked steps. It has never claimed to be a speakeasy. It's just an intimate bar that most of the tourists walking up and down SoCo will never know about (until they read this book!)

Available for walk-ins and reservations, the dark space features a few cozy lounge areas with leather seating and wood walls. My favorite place to sit is right at the bar. I love to grab a barstool, talk to the bartenders about the various whiskies that I might not have heard of, and watch them carefully craft a cocktail. The menu of exclusive Japanese whiskies, sake, and seasonal craft cocktails is curated with care. Watertrade guests get the added benefit of being able to order bar bites from the accompanying 12-seat sushi counter, Otoko, for which dinner tickets cost several hundred dollars per person. Since that might be aspirational for

those who just spent the day eating and shopping on SoCo, Watertrade is an excellent entry point (both literally and figuratively) to the full *omakase* experience.

Since Watertrade is a bit off the beaten path, you'll find that most of the other guests are also there for an evening of exceptional cocktails or exclusive Japanese whisky. This is a bar for people who want a quiet, elevated evening with a friend in a beautiful setting.

Like I mentioned, Watertrade is the entry point to Otoko, one of the most exclusive *omakase* sushi counters in Austin. Otoko is an excellent "bonus" dinner spot to add to your day on South Congress. But, since I've already given you several other options for food, we'll just leave this as a nightcap and bid farewell to South Congress.

THE BOULDIN CREEK CRAWL

1. Start your morning with a homemade vegetarian breakfast at **BOULDIN CREEK CAFE**, 1900 S. 1ST ST., AUSTIN, (512) 416-1601, BOULDINCREEKCAFE.COM

2. Brunch with the peacocks at **MATTIE'S AT GREEN PASTURES**, 811 W. LIVE OAK ST., AUSTIN, (512) 444-1888, MATTIESAUSTIN.COM

3. Indulge in award-winning cupcakes at **SUGAR MAMA'S BAKESHOP**, 1905 S. 1ST ST., AUSTIN, (512) 448-3727, SUGARMAMASBAKESHOP.COM

4. Soak up the south Austin vibes at **FRESA'S CHICKEN AL CARBON**, 1703 S. 1ST ST., AUSTIN, (512) 992-2946, FRESASCHICKEN.COM

5. Savor authentic Thai cuisine at neighborhood café **THAI FRESH**, 909 W. MARY ST., AUSTIN, (512) 494-6436, THAI-FRESH.COM

6. Pair pizza and craft cocktails at **DOVETAIL**, 1816 S. 1ST ST., AUSTIN, (512) 522-1375, DOVETAILPIZZA.COM

7. Cozy up next to your date at **LENOIR**, 1807 S. 1ST ST., AUSTIN, (512) 215-9778, LENOIRRESTAURANT.COM

8. End your night with a scoop of authentic Italian gelato at **DOLCE NEVE GELATO**, 1713 S. 1ST ST., AUSTIN, (512) 804-5568, DOLCENEVEGELATO.COM

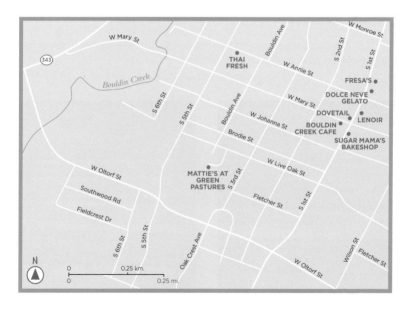

Bouldin Creek

Austin's Last Hidden Gem

OK OK . . . ASK ANYONE WHO'S SEARCHING FOR REAL ESTATE IN this area and they won't say it's a "hidden gem." Prices have been soaring in the last decade! And for good reason. This walkable neighborhood is tucked in-between Zilker Park on the west (Austin City Limits Music Festival, Barton Springs Pool), and South Congress on the east (helllooooo tourists!). It's an incredibly convenient location in the heart of south Austin and many people want to call it home, but Bouldin Creek often gets overlooked by tourists who are visiting Austin and looking for the best places to hang out for a day of eating and drinking. I'm going to try to convince you otherwise. When folks think "Austin, Texas," this neighborhood is often what they envision: old Mexican bakeries next to grungy tattoo parlors, hip little wine bars with sprawling patios decked out with twinkly lights, hodgepodge streets of houses with both 1950s bungalows and modern rebuilds, decades-old graffiti, small sidewalks shaded by live oak trees, and cash-only food trucks with lines of customers. Being only a mile from downtown, Bouldin Creek has become one of the most desirable residential neighborhoods in Austin. Bouldin Creek is funky, quirky, and constantly evolving.

Many Bouldin Creek restaurants can be found on South First Street, which is considered the younger, quieter sister to the iconic South Congress Avenue just a few blocks away. Never fear: Although smaller and less crowded, South First boasts an equally impressive number of restaurants, bars, bakeries, food trucks, and breweries. Plan on a full day of eating, starting with breakfast, lunch, dessert, moving to happy hour and dinner, and maybe saving a little space for a late-night scoop of gelato.

1

START YOUR MORNING WITH A HOMEMADE VEGETARIAN BREAKFAST AT BOULDIN CREEK CAFE

Vegetarians and meat-eaters alike sprawl out in the hot Texas sun, waiting in the hours-long queue for a table at **BOULDIN CREEK CAFE**'s weekend breakfast. And although Sunday is the busiest meal of the week, that chipotle-pecan pesto can even make a Monday morning just a little bit brighter. This place is buzzing with south Austin vibes, starting with the "Caffeine Dealer" sign flashing toward South First Street.

This old-school Austin cafe serves omelets, sandwiches, break-fast tacos, and pastries for anyone who just wants good, homemade food. Yes, you can order dairy and eggs here, but even if you're not following a vegan lifestyle, try the tofu scramble at least once. You won't be sorry. And if you're over-whelmed by all the options in the pastry case, start with that giant,

soft oatmeal cream sandwich cookie for a tasty vegan treat.

The drink menu offers locally roasted fair-trade coffee and over 20 varieties of tea, and the words Hangover Helper! in bright red illuminate the drink options for those who had just a little too much fun last night and need things like coconut water and Emergen-C. The indoor bar area is buzzing from morning to night. Early risers get a caffeine fix to start the day, and the folks stop by during afternoon happy hour for great deals on beer and wine.

Although Bouldin Creek Cafe is a wonderful breakfast spot for those who want to experience true south Austin, it is in no way a tourist trap. The same local customers come back week after week, year after year, eager to catch up with friends and indulge in homemade, hearty, healthy food.

Next up: another south Austin hotspot where you'll want to make your brunch reservations weeks in advance.

2 BRUNCH WITH THE PEACOCKS AT MATTIE'S AT GREEN PASTURES

Most people don't expect to see peacocks in a central Texas city, but step onto **MATTIE'S** lawn and you'll witness a muster of long-tailed white and bright-blue birds strutting on the grassy carpet, proudly displaying their feathers. The peacocks are only one of the reasons why wandering onto Mattie's property feels a bit like walking into another world.

Unlike most Bouldin Creek restaurants, which are on South First Street, Mattie's is nestled between houses in a residential neighborhood. The mansion, built around 1895, was originally home to Martha "Mattie" Faulk, and her husband, Henry. Though the original restaurant, Green Pastures, has recently been updated and renamed, the bones of the house remain. As does the famous 1965 Milk Punch on the cocktail menu. It's a creamy, booze-filled treat with sweet cream, bourbon and rum, maple, and a sprinkle of fresh nutmeg on top.

The multilevel interior has grand windows, creaking wooden floors, and lots of rooms for dining space. The lawn is a darling place to gather with your brunch party, order a cocktail, and kick off the weekend with a delicious Southern meal.

Mattie's offers spruced-up versions of classic Southern dishes. Start with their light and fluffy buttermilk biscuits with seasonal butter and local honey, and be sure to try the famous Mattie's Fried Chicken, either

as an entree for dinner or in a fried chicken eggs Benedict version for brunch.

Enjoy dessert here, or mosey on to the next stop to order some of Austin's favorite cupcakes.

Mattie's Famous 1965 Milk Punch

Mattie's beverage director Jason Stevens resurrected the original 1965 milk punch recipe, using only highest quality booze, rich, fresh milk, and freshly grated nutmeg.

Ingredients:
4 ounces Buffalo Trace
    bourbon
3 ounces Pierre Ferrand
    1840 cognac
1½ ounces Appleton
    Reserve Jamaican rum
16 ounces half and half
8 ounces whole milk
2½ ounces grade A or B
    maple syrup
2 ounces Tempus Fugit
    crème de cacao
1 ounce quality vanilla
    paste
Whole nutmeg, for grating

Directions:
Combine all ingredients except for the nutmeg in a pitcher and stir vigorously to make sure the vanilla is fully dispersed in the mix.

Serve very cold. Dispense 1965 Milk Punch into small, chilled cups and then grate fresh nutmeg over each serving.

Recipe makes enough to serve a group of 4–6.

3

INDULGE IN AWARD-WINNING CUPCAKES AT SUGAR MAMA'S BAKESHOP

The cupcake craze took the United States by storm in the early 2000s. And while some massive cupcake chains did not manage to survive, **SUGAR MAMA'S** is still thriving and selling out of popular cupcake flavors daily.

And that's probably because chef Olivia O'Neal, who won first place on Cupcake Wars in 2013, still insists that Sugar Mama's makes absolutely everything from scratch. Waltz into the small bakery in south Austin and enjoy the scent of sugar, butter, and vanilla that hits you right when you walk through the front door. The classic cupcake flavors are the best place to start. Order a James (Valrhona chocolate cake topped with chocolate buttercream and sprinkles) or a classic Beckett (buttery vanilla cupcakes with Madagascar bourbon vanilla buttercream) with a hot cup of coffee.

Sugar Mama's does cupcakes really well, but it's a full-blown bakery, too. Pies, cookies, cakes, and bars also take up a hefty amount of space in the pastry case. The custom cake orders are perfect for birthdays and other special occasions.

The only complaint I have about Sugar Mama's is that I get too full before I get to taste all the cupcakes! My solution? Order a bunch, cut them into small pieces, and share with a group of friends.

"We opened Sugar Mama's Bakeshop in 2008 when Austin was on the verge of becoming the food-centric town it has evolved into. We opened with front-of-house experience, but very little back-of-house experience, and we had to learn as we went along!

"It has been both exciting and challenging to be a part of the food revolution here in the Bouldin Creek neighborhood. From the beginning we have had a focus on utilizing local (when possible), fair trade, and gourmet ingredients in all of our desserts. We are proud that we have never had to compromise in this area due to the ongoing support of the community in patronizing our business."

—*Olivia O'Neal,*
chef and owner of
Sugar Mama's Bakeshop

4

SOAK UP THE SOUTH AUSTIN VIBES AT FRESA'S CHICKEN AL CARBON

Prickly pear margaritas, creekside patio dining, grilled chicken platters, and scratch-made gourmet ice cream . . . it doesn't get much better than **FRESA'S CHICKEN AL CARBON**. Whether you stop by the walk-up window for breakfast tacos or indulge in a full meal during sunset, be sure to add Fresa's to your Bouldin Creek food crawl.

This restaurant is all about chicken: bowls, platters, tacos, and salads. The charred, smoky bits are the best part, and you can order your chicken with various flavor profiles, like achiote and citrus, or Yucatan spice. Most people think of chicken as the healthy/boring meat, and things like pork belly or steak or upscale seafood as the fun stuff. But go ahead and reset your expectations, because the grilled chicken at Fresa's is just so yummy, you're going to be craving it again and again.

And don't forget about those sides! The grilled sweet potatoes with arbol chile oil and cilantro are quite literally what dreams are made of. (Yes, I've actually had a dream about these sweet potatoes, and no, it won't seem weird to you once you try them.) They're charred and caramelized on the outside, and pillowy soft on the outside. Dunk them in the poblano ranch dipping sauce and then take a sip of that frozen prickly pear margarita, and muah *chef's kiss.* Perfection.

From the fully loaded queso and Mexican street corn, served on the cob, to the hearty and healthy salads and bowls, Fresa's is that go-to restaurant in Austin that's perfect for nearly any occasion. I love this place for a casual dinner celebration, like a group birthday party or a big family gathering. There are large outdoor tables on the patio, and the giant trees overhead and nearby creek provide the perfect Austin ambience.

Final tip: You must order the ice cream for dessert. "Wait, ice cream at a grilled chicken restaurant?" you ask? Yes. The ice cream program was originally created by pastry chef and James Beard Award semifinalist Laura Sawicki. The flavors change seasonally, but favorites like lemon meringue pie, chocolate coconut, and Rice Krispie treat keep coming back.

5

SAVOR AUTHENTIC THAI CUISINE AT NEIGHBORHOOD CAFÉ THAI FRESH

There's hardly anything more "Austin-y" than this little neighborhood Thai restaurant and bakery tucked into a small street in Bouldin Creek. THAI FRESH opened in 2008 and hasn't changed a whole lot since then. Why not? Because they don't need to.

The owner, Jam, who is from Bangkok, started cooking at age 5. The menu features her recipes and cooking methods.

The menu is fairly robust, but a good rule of thumb is to pick one starter + one noodle or curry dish. The traditional Thai chicken wings are a good place to start. They're satisfying and delicious, mixed with garlic, cilantro, and peppercorn, or tossed with a sticky Sriracha honey garlic sauce. If it's a cold day in Austin and I want something comforting, the *tom kha* coconut soup is rich and creamy with a kick of spice. For entrees, the classic pad thai is the bestseller here. They make so many orders of it! The chewy noodles are slightly sweet, a bit tangy from the fish sauce, and the perfect bed for a protein of your choice. I'm not vegetarian, but the bricks of seared

tofu are my go-to, every time. The red curry *kaeng ped* is delightfully spicy, full of dried chiles and topped with a heap of fresh Thai basil.

Perhaps the most wonderful part of Thai Fresh is their pastry case, which is overflowing with gluten-free and (mostly) vegan desserts. Of course, you don't have to follow a gluten-free or vegan lifestyle to enjoy these pastries; they're all decadent and sweet, and served in large portions. I love their salty caramel brownie. Ask for it to be heated up! Their bars and brownies, giant vegan cookies, and delicious fluffy vanilla bean sour cream coffee cake are other favorites.

I could easily fill a page just telling you how much I adore the pastries at Thai Fresh, but I'll just let you stop by and try them for yourself. Next up is another neighborhood spot that will probably make you want to move to Bouldin Creek just so you can walk here on a regular basis.

6

PAIR PIZZA AND CRAFT COCKTAILS AT DOVETAIL

DOVETAIL is an adorable neighborhood pizza restaurant that's made to be enjoyed with your friends. While the pizza style here doesn't really follow any strict guidelines, it's somewhere between Neapolitan and NY-style; the dough is slowly fermented to give it that rich chewiness. The pies are big and oval-shaped, served on a rectangular cookie sheet, and made to be shared with your table.

This is a totally casual spot. I've meandered in around 5:30 p.m. for an early dinner with the kids, and I've stopped by for a late meal at the bar with a friend before going downtown for a concert. If you crave great cocktails, friendly hospitality, and delicious Italian-inspired food, Dovetail needs to be on your list.

Start with their baked ricotta, made in-house and served with their slightly sweet butternut squash ricotta and delightfully thick-cut garlic bread. A yummy salad with fresh, crisp produce can round out your starters.

Oh, wait . . . we need to back up to drinks! Dovetail isn't fussy, but that doesn't mean they don't know how to make a mean Negroni. The small-yet-mighty wine list features wine by the glass or bottle, including everything from predictable classics like an Italian pinot grigio or a rich barbera, as well as unusual options like unfiltered bottles and orange wine.

Both the pizza and pasta shine here, so go with whatever your heart desires. If you're dining with a big group and can order a bunch of things,

lucky you! Try their spaghetti and meatball (yes, one meatball . . . but it's huge), the incredible chicken parm, or a classic pepperoni pizza with three types of cheeses.

Grab a scoop of that soft-serve ice cream and you'll be on your way!

Looking for a more formal date night dinner in Bouldin Creek? Make reservations for our next stop and get ready to enjoy one of the best meals in Austin.

7

COZY UP NEXT TO YOUR DATE AT LENOIR

New American fare in a rustic chic setting makes **LENOIR** one of the most desirable and intimate dinner reservations in Austin. The restaurant can be broken into two parts: the small indoor dining room, which seats about 30, and the larger backyard wine garden.

Lenoir is located inside a tiny bungalow house. If you think it looks tiny from the outside, step inside and you'll see . . . you are correct. The interior dining room is snug and cozy. I have a theory that it is quite impossible to feel any stress at all while on Lenoir's property.

Lenoir's team is committed to sourcing from local Texas farmers, butchers, and winemakers. Chef Todd Duplechan's "hot weather food" is meant to be grown, raised, and consumed in Texas. Guests can enjoy entrees a la carte, or a prix-fixe menu with wine pairings.

The outdoor wine garden is larger than the indoor dining area, though equally rustic and endearing. Lanterns and lights hang from decades-old live oak trees, illuminating white wooden tables and benches on a gravel floor. The full menu is available in this outdoor

dining space, and heaters, fans, misters, and tents are available to make sure you can dine outdoors at any time of the year. If you're in Austin in the most beautiful months (October and November, March and April), I highly recommend requesting a table in Lenoir's backyard. If it's a cold winter evening or an exceptionally hot summer day, the indoor restaurant space is incredibly romantic and beautiful.

I'm an introvert, so I thrive on small gatherings with just one or two people from my group of friends. One of my happiest places is sitting in Lenoir's wine garden, sharing a bottle of bubbles and farmer veggies and *labneh* with friends on a hot summer night.

8

END YOUR NIGHT WITH A SCOOP OF AUTHENTIC ITALIAN GELATO AT DOLCE NEVE GELATO

In a city that experiences summer weather for about 75 percent of the year, a good gelato shop is a must. Thankfully, a sweet trio of Italians decided to open a shop in Bouldin Creek that offers the best gelato you'll find in town.

DOLCE NEVE

local·italian·gelato

The phrase "We do it in front of everyone" is displayed at the entrance for all to see. Directly underneath the sign, store employees are often churning fresh batches of gelato, sorbet, waffle cones, and other frozen snacks to serve each day.

Don't be surprised by the teeny sizes offered; gelato is dense, tightly packed into the small cups, and a little goes a long way. A combination of staples, rotating flavors, and seasonal flavors entice curious customers who stumble into the tiny, bright building. My personal favorite flavors? Anything with cheese: *fromage blanc,* goat cheese, ricotta, or mascarpone!

Authentic Italian gelato should meet a few criteria, and Dolce Neve checks everything off this list:

Natural flavors and colors. If you see oddly bright colors that wouldn't naturally occur from the ingredients (like bright green mint or hot pink strawberry gelato), they probably used artificial coloring.

Gelato that's stored in metal tins with lids, which help regulate the temperature of the delicate dessert. Gelato, which is made with a lower fat content than ice cream, has to be served slightly warmer. To ensure the optimal temperatures, a great gelato shop like Dolce Neve stores the cold treat at a careful temperature. (Beware of those big fluffy mounds showcased behind glass; they're probably full of artificial fillers.)

Traditional flavors (think: *stracciatella,* pistachio, chocolate), as well as a few unique ones.

THE ZILKER CRAWL

1. Order Austin's best coffee and scones at **PATIKA**, 2159 S. LAMAR BLVD., AUSTIN, PATIKACOFFEE.COM

2. Lunch at **CHI'LANTRO BBQ**, home of the original kimchi fries, 1509 S. LAMAR BLVD., AUSTIN, (512) 428-5269, CHILANTROBBQ.COM

3. Slurp a bowl of noodles at **RAMEN TATSU-YA**, 1234 S. LAMAR BLVD., AUSTIN, (512) 893-5561, RAMEN-TATSUYA.COM

4. Sip a sake slushee at **LORO ASIAN SMOKEHOUSE**, 2115 S. LAMAR BLVD., AUSTIN, (512) 916-4858, LOROEATS.COM/LOCATIONS/AUSTIN/SOUTH-LAMAR

5. Plan the perfect farm-to-table meal at **ODD DUCK**, 1201 S. LAMAR BLVD., AUSTIN, (512) 433-6512, ODDDUCKAUSTIN.COM

6. Live music, food trucks, and beer at **RADIO COFFEE AND BEER**, 4204 MANCHACA RD., AUSTIN, (512) 394-7844, RADIOCOFFEEAND BEER.COM

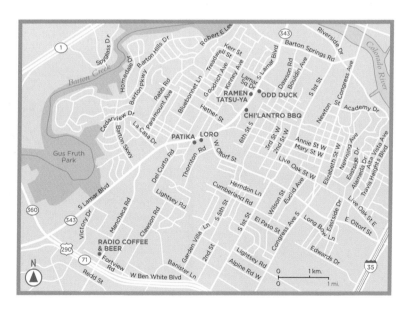

Zilker

Austin City Limits and Barton Springs Pool

THINK OF ZILKER PARK AS AUSTIN'S VERSION OF CENTRAL PARK.
It's our greenspace, our playground, hangout spot, and our "jewel in the heart of Austin." Zilker Park is home to Austin City Limits Music Festival every October, a 1-acre spring-fed pool, stand-up paddleboarding, a sculpture garden, a hike-and-bike path, and an unobstructed view of the Austin skyline. And since you'll most likely be in this area at some point for ACL Fest, Barton Springs Pool, or just to hang out and play soccer at the park, the Zilker neighborhood is a great place to enjoy a day of eating and drinking.

South Lamar is the main north/south street in Zilker, and it's absolutely packed with great coffee shops, restaurants, and food trucks. I'll be sure to include plenty of places to get caffeinated and fuel up before the festival, and a bunch of casual spots where you can grab some food in the evening when you're ready to unwind.

Like pretty much all of Austin, Zilker has experienced a boom of real estate development in the last decade. But old Austin charm still shines through amid the glitzy, high-rise apartments and mixed-use developments.

Here's an example: Far down south at the end of South Lamar, just before the street runs into Ben White Boulevard, you'll find a small country dance hall called The Broken Spoke. It's squeezed between two towering mixed-use developments that offer living, retail, and work space. Although the space around The Broken Spoke is constantly evolving, the building and the clientele have hardly changed since it opened in 1964; it's still Austin's favorite place to dress in western wear, two-step, and drink Shiner Bock. What has changed, though, is that you can now leave the dance hall and find world-renowned restaurants, coffee shops, food trucks, and bars on South Lamar Boulevard.

1

ORDER AUSTIN'S BEST COFFEE AND SCONES AT PATIKA

I drove past this tiny 1940s building many times before noticing it and deciding to stop in. PATIKA is inside what used to be an old tax building, meticulously renovated to create a charming, midcentury modern space for coffee, conversation, and delicious food.

Their sister company, Superthing, roasts the coffee beans. They search all over the world for the most interesting coffee beans, carefully sourcing them from sustainable farmers and growers, and geek out over roasting them and creating the best coffee you've ever tried. One of my favorite parts about getting a cup of coffee at Patika is grabbing a bag of coffee beans with my order. I'll chat with the barista about tasting notes and flavor profiles, because the baristas at Patika are highly skilled and true coffee nerds . . . in the best possible way.

Ok, but I've been chatting far too long about the coffee without getting to the important stuff: THE PASTRIES. Yes, Patika is darling and has one of the best coffee programs in Austin, and yes, you can indulge in a full, delicious breakfast or brunch meal here. But without a doubt, no matter what, even if you're not a coffee drinker, you absolutely must stop by Patika and get one of their scones!

Why are they so good? They're homemade with lots of real butter. They're not that sickly sugary/frosted version you might get at a drive-thru coffee chain . . . they're dense and tall with a hint of sweetness. And

the flavors are superior to pretty much any other pastry case flavors you've tasted: blueberry basil, vanilla lavender, chocolate cherry, and mango chili lime, among many others. The flavors rotate and the pastry case typically has about two scone flavors and three muffin flavors at a time. Whenever I see the banana graham muffin, I make sure to order one.

Whether you need a large coffee and a french toast muffin to go, or you plan to sit and connect with someone over a leisurely brunch of *shakshuka* toast or some biscuits and chorizo poblano gravy, Patika is the perfect place to kick off your morning in the Zilker neighborhood of south Austin.

And for lunch? Let's head to Austin's favorite mini chain, which started out as a food truck way back in the day.

2 LUNCH AT CHI'LANTRO BBQ, HOME OF THE ORIGINAL KIMCHI FRIES

There's a history in Austin of a food truck opening up, seizing the city's attention by cooking excellent, creative food, and then turning into a successful brick and mortar business with multiple locations. Example: **CHI'LANTRO**.

Korean barbecue meets Mexican food at this fusion-fare hotspot on SoLa. They're "Home of the Original Kimchi Fries," which are an absolute must-try menu item for the first-time customer. What exactly are kimchi fries, you ask? Chi'Lantro starts with a heap of thick fries, covers them with your choice of protein (spicy pork or chicken, soy-glazed chicken, tofu, or Korean barbecue steak), and tops the whole thing with caramelized kimchi, cheese, onions, cilantro, magic sauce, sesame seeds, and Sriracha. It's a completely justifiable way to count fries as a complete meal.

Other favorites are the popular tacos, bowls, queso, and wings; they all take a basic concept and spin it through a mix of cultures to create a delectable, memorable, completely Insta-worthy meal. The Chi'Jeu Queso with the optional soy-glazed chicken (it's optional, but . . . it's really not!) is a must-order menu item.

This food truck has expanded into a business with several brick and mortars, so you can find Chi'Lantro locations all over the city.

Throwback story: My husband and I love the kimchi fries so much, we decided to hire the food truck to serve them for dinner at our 2017 wedding. This was back when the Chi'Lantro food truck was still willing to drive all over Austin to cater various events. Seeing that food truck roll up to my wedding to serve my guests one of my favorite Austin meals was one of the many highlights of that evening!

Chi'Lantro is great on any day of the year, but if it's cold and rainy today, you 100 percent need to stop at the next restaurant on this food crawl.

3

SLURP A BOWL OF NOODLES AT RAMEN TATSU-YA

Austin has become the proud home to all sorts of types of ramen, with thin, thick, or curly noodles, from velvety rich *tonkotsu* pork bone broth to subtle shio chicken-based broth, *tsukemen* dipping noodles, and even vegetarian and vegan variations.

But if you just have time for one bowl of ramen, and you're not sure where to go, here's my best suggestion: Stop by **RAMEN TATSU-YA** on your journey through Zilker.

What makes this place so special? Co-owners Tatsu Aikawa and Takuya "Tako" Matsumoto take pride in their specialty: *tonkotsu*. This is a creamy ramen from Kyushu, Japan, which simmers up to 60 hours in order to summon the flavors of each ingredient. Pork fat permeates every ounce of broth, making this giant bowl of broth and noodles one of the most delectable comfort foods you can find in Austin.

When you're ready to order, there are several options. *Tonkotsu* is Tatsu-Ya's strong suit; Tatsu and Tako spent months perfecting the complexities of the broth, noodles, and toppings. From there, you might wish to venture to the *Tonkotsu-Shoyu*, which adds a decadent soy sauce blend to the pork bone broth, or try a Mi-So-

Is your ramen vocabulary ready for Tatsu-Ya?

Tonkotsu: A rich, slow-cooked broth made from simmering pork bones and fat. Not to be confused with tonkatsu, a popular fried pork cutlet dish.

Shio: A clear, thin broth with salt added.

Miso: A fermented soybean broth, typically paired with heavy meat like pork; can also be spicy.

Chashu: Soy-braised pork belly.

Kikurage: Wood-ear mushroom.

Not (mild) or Mi-So-Hot (spicy) for a broth made with fermented soybean.

Broth and noodles are the stars of the show, but ramen is more exciting with some fun toppings; try ordering several to find your own personal favorites! Certain toppings come standard at Tatsu-Ya, like the chashu (soy-braised pork belly) and *ajitama* (marinated soft-boiled egg), but I also like to add a spicy bomb of red pepper paste, corn with brown butter, and an extra sheet of nori.

4

SIP A SAKE SLUSHEE AT LORO ASIAN SMOKEHOUSE

Two of Austin's most beloved chefs (Tyson Cole, Uchi, and Aaron Franklin, Franklin Barbecue) put their superpowers together to create **LORO ASIAN SMOKEHOUSE** on South Lamar. I've eaten here with my spouse for date night, I've met up with a big group of girlfriends for a casual outdoor dinner, and I've even stopped by solo for a drink and a bite at the bar. This is that "it's-delicious-at-any-occasion" type of spot. In fact, Loro is so popular, they've even opened additional locations in other Texas cities!

The dog-friendly patio is the place to be on a warm Austin evening. Start your meal with one of those boozy slushees, like the mango sake slushee, a refreshing frozen gin and tonic, or even a flight of three flavors of your choice.

Loro cooks their meat low and slow, the same way you would expect any upstanding Texas barbecue restaurant to do it. They smoke the meat overnight so it's ready for lunch the next day, which means you and I can indulge in

melt-in-your-mouth brisket, perfectly juicy smoked turkey, and a decadent *char siew* pork belly by lunch time. Of course, all of the meat, sandwiches, rice bowls, and salads are fused with Asian flavors, like oak-smoked beef brisket served with papaya salad and Thai herbs. Even the bar snacks are fascinating. Be sure to try the wonton chips and dip with thai green salsa and peanut sambal.

5

PLAN THE PERFECT FARM-TO-TABLE MEAL AT ODD DUCK

Bryce Gilmore, owner of **ODD DUCK**, is one of the pioneers of the farm-to-table movement in Austin. His mission to source seasonally from local farmers led to his opening a "farm-to-trailer" food truck in 2009, which eventually grew the gorgeous brick and mortar Odd Duck in 2013.

The rustic charm of the restaurant matches the farm-to-table concept: Burlap-wrapped chandeliers hang from the ceiling and food is served on mismatched vintage dishware. The large central bar, kitchen, and prep space fill up the majority of the restaurant, with a smattering of tables around the perimeter and outdoor dining available.

Odd Duck's mission now is the same as it was at the very beginning: to use locally sourced food and to prepare it beautifully. It seems like a simple concept now, but back when the food truck was just getting started, sustainability wasn't such a hot topic and it was

a pretty radical idea. Odd Duck was a major player in putting Austin on the map as a destination food city, which is why I always recommend that people make a dinner reservation here for one of their first meals in Austin, either as a visitor or as a resident.

I love to start my meal with whatever bread variation they're offering. The last time I was there, it was a cast iron cornbread with sweet potato chili butter. The fresh and local seafood dishes are always phenomenal, like the salt and pepper head-on shrimp with hot shiitake sweet and sour sauce and porkonaise. Both the starters and the larger dishes at the bottom of the menu are meant to be shared, which is great by me—I love to try a little bit of everything! Stuffed quail with pickled onion and hot sauce jus, grilled wagyu strip with steak sauce and turnip green fritters, and an aged wagyu burger with pinto beans and fried egg queso are just a few examples of items you might find on Odd Duck's menu.

The menu changes by the seasons (and often by the day), so I can't recommend a specific item. But you know you'll always get whatever is fresh and local! If you're stumped by the menu, ask your server for recommendations, or look at the photos on Odd Duck's Instagram account (@oddduck austin) for stunning shots of the latest and greatest menu items.

6

LIVE MUSIC, FOOD TRUCKS, AND BEER AT RADIO COFFEE AND BEER

Follow South Lamar until it splits into two roads, and follow the eastern road, Manchaca, until you eventually run into a hybrid coffee shop and beer garden. It's nestled under a shady grove of trees that provides a canopy over the sprawling outdoor patio, and it's consistently crowded with regulars.

Folks gather at **RADIO COFFEE AND BEER** morning, noon, and night for caffeine, beer, live music, food trucks, and a comfortable gathering place to meet up with friends. The renovated house provides a cool space for working quietly on a laptop, joining a group for trivia night, and listening to a bluegrass band play on the small corner stage.

Radio is an all-day coffee shop and bar, which means they have drinks for any hour of the day. A full coffee bar will get you started with a caffeine kick in the morning. Meeting a buddy in the afternoon? Get some kombucha or nitro cold brew on tap. For folks who visit Radio at night, the beer selection provides a peek into the vast craft beer scene in Austin. Try pours from popular Austin breweries like St. Elmo, Pinthouse, and Austin Beerworks. Radio also has a huge selection of cocktails (I love their spicy margarita in the summertime), wine, and non-alcoholic options.

Another huge draw of Radio, of course, is the selection of food trucks parked outside. The food trucks are mostly permanent, but they occasionally rotate them out. You can most likely expect to find a great place to get street tacos, some crazy good Thai food, and a really solid breakfast sandwich. But check their website to see what they have available at the moment.

THE CESAR CHAVEZ CRAWL

1. Fuel your weekend with a hearty ranch-to-table brunch at **JACOBY'S RESTAURANT AND MERCANTILE**, 3235 E. CESAR CHAVEZ ST., AUSTIN, (512) 366-5808, JACOBYSAUSTIN.COM

2. Eat award-winning cuisine in a renovated laundromat at **LAUNDERETTE**, 2115 HOLLY ST., AUSTIN, (512) 382-1599, LAUNDERETTEAUSTIN.COM

3. Escape to Mexico City at **DE NADA CANTINA**, 4715 E. CESAR CHAVEZ ST., AUSTIN, (512) 615-3555, DENADACANTINA.COM

4. It's a permanent vacation at **HOLIDAY ON 7TH**, 5020 E. 7TH ST., AUSTIN, HOLIDAYON7TH.COM

5. Pretend you're in Italy with Neapolitan-style pies at **BUFALINA**, 2215 E. CESAR CHAVEZ ST., AUSTIN, (512) 394-5337, BUFALINAPIZZA.COM

6. Sneak away to a sultry date night at **JUSTINE'S BRASSERIE**, 4710 E. 5TH ST., AUSTIN, (512) 385-2900, JUSTINES1937.COM

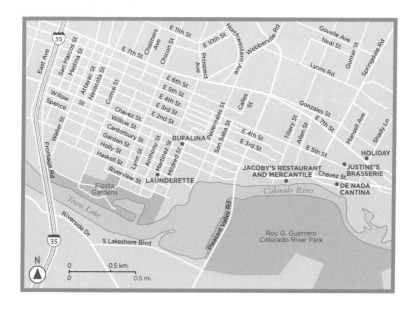

Cesar Chavez

Tacos, Beer, and Fun Patios

EAST AUSTIN IS MASSIVE, AND A BIT OVERWHELMING. YOU COULD spend weeks (months?) eating your way through this food playground. We're going to start by covering one of the densest restaurant streets in Austin: Cesar Chavez.

Named after the American civil rights activist, this area has experienced rapid growth in the past decade. It's one of Austin's oldest neighborhoods, and now one of the hottest areas to live, eat, and hang out. Although it's just a few blocks from downtown, Cesar Chavez still has a neighborhood vibe, making this a popular place for locals to live and visitors to stay in boutique hotels or vacation rentals. And since the area is still very residential, you're going to have a lot of fun walking your way through this day of eating. As the population density has increased, so have the restaurant choices. Sure, Cesar Chavez is still a great place to find the Austin classics, like taco shops, dive bars, and barbecue food trucks. But the area also includes farm-to-table fare, trendy pizzerias, and restaurants from award-winning chefs. I've listed six of the best options for eating and drinking your way down Cesar Chavez, but rest assured that there are many other fun neighborhood gems that you might stumble upon as you explore. Get your eating pants ready!

1

FUEL YOUR WEEKEND WITH A HEARTY RANCH-TO-TABLE BRUNCH AT JACOBY'S RESTAURANT AND MERCANTILE

JACOBY'S ranch-to-table restaurant is just about as "Texas" of a dining experience as you can find. Owned by husbands Kris Swift and Adam Jacoby, Jacoby's Restaurant originally started as a Feed and Seed in 1981 and has grown into a vertically integrated business. Here's what that means: You're sitting at the darling Jacoby's Restaurant and Mercantile in east Austin, eating a juicy cheeseburger, which was made with Jacoby's beef, from an animal raised on Jacoby's ranch, which was fed Jacoby's own specially mixed finishing ration, which was made by Jacoby's Feed and Seed. No need to question how the meat was raised or sourced! The ½ pound cheeseburger at Jacoby's is one of the best in town, and the migas plate is a feast of smoked chicken, queso, ranchero, sour cream, scrambled eggs, crunchy house chips, and pico. Another crowd favorite, the chicken-fried steak and waffles, is covered in homemade sausage gravy and maple syrup, because this is brunch, my friend, and there's no need to skimp.

Of course, there are plenty of menu items for folks who aren't interested in meat. Head to the "SWEET" section of the menu for a list of

french toast, cakes, and scones, all made in-house. The sweets menu might rotate, except for one constant item: Grandma Hager's strawberry cake. There is something so classically Southern about a slice of light pink cake covered with a thick layer of strawberry frosting. The most recent time I brunched here, I ordered an apple knot with pecan icing to share with the table. Needless to say, I immediately regretted not getting my own. The smoked cheese grits with Cajun butter and pickled peppers are, however, a nice menu item to share with friends. They're rich and cheesy, perfect for sneaking in small bites to accompany your choice of entree. And the maple pecan pancakes, topped with whipped cream and maple syrup, are a hearty, decadent option for an entree or a shareable plate. Bacon is listed as an option for the pancakes, but is it really an option? As we've already established: Brunch is not a time to cut corners.

A food crawl is all about indulging, so we're going to head to another one of my all-time favorite East Austin restaurants for some eats and drinks.

2 EAT AWARD-WINNING CUISINE IN A RENOVATED LAUNDROMAT AT LAUNDERETTE

LAUNDERETTE is worth every bit of hype it has received. You might have heard of this restaurant from its multiple James Beard Foundation Award nominations, or from its accolades in Food & Wine or Texas Monthly. This New American restaurant is in one of the most unusual restaurant buildings in Austin: a renovated laundromat and gas station. The interior is sleek and trendy, and the large patio makes a lovely place to enjoy a leisurely lunch with a group of pals. Many of the plates here are meant to be shared; chef Rene Ortiz has created a fun mix of cultures with his snacky starters, showstopping vegetable plates, and wood-grilled entrees. Some of the menu items will rotate, but plan on starting with a few small bites for the table. I love the bright

beet hummus with *labneh* or the homemade potato chips and pimento cheese. The crab and avocado toast on semolina bread is heaped high with bold flavors; there is no shame in ordering toast for dinner when it tastes this good. The brick chicken, served on a bed of sauce *aligot* and braised greens, is a must-try item. Don't be fooled by the simple name; this piece of tender chicken in a flavorful, crisp crust is a showstopper and crowd favorite. And, of course, the *plancha* burger is considered one of the best in Austin. Don't forget to add *frites* and garlic aioli!

Launderette's desserts shouldn't be considered an afterthought. Some people come here for desserts alone! The birthday cake ice cream sandwich is an iconic Austin menu item that tastes just as good as it looks on Instagram. Imaginative icebox pies, parfaits, cakes, and sorbets are prepared with a delicate balance of flavor and elaborate plating skills. I once made the mistake of leaving Launderette without ordering dessert, and that will never happen again.

3 ESCAPE TO MEXICO CITY AT DE NADA CANTINA

When someone asks you if you want to go out for happy hour tacos and margaritas, you should immediately suggest **DE NADA CANTINA**.

(And then cross your fingers you can manage to get a table!) This Mexico City–style taqueria serves just a few things, but they do them really well.

De Nada makes house-made blue corn tortillas that are soft and fresh, every single day. They use these to make delicious small tacos, filled with slow-braised meat, spicy salsa, and grilled veggies. Round out your meal with some chips and the De Nada Trio (queso, guacamole, and salsa) and devour. Pair your meal with a couple hand-shaken margaritas

or another specialty cocktail (I'm a big fan of their spicy pineapple with mezcal and Ancho Reyes Verde), and enjoy the perfect meal with friends or family on one of their multiple patios.

De Nada has a lot of unique furniture and textiles that are directly from Mexico, including a beautiful fountain in the front. This restaurant feels like you're stepping into a different city, and I think that's part of the reason it's been so popular in Austin. Everyone wants to feel like they're on vacation!

Speaking of vacation, the next stop is 100 percent going to feel like you're on holiday. It's even in the name.

4

IT'S A PERMANENT VACATION AT HOLIDAY ON 7TH

I bet you'll never guess what this place used to be by looking at it! Let's see . . . sprawling back patio, modern white interior, a beautiful horse-shoe-shaped bar that's always crowded with regulars . . . ding ding! You're right, HOLIDAY was a former auto body shop. Ok, I'm obviously joking here, because this renovated space feels festive and feminine and NOTHING like the old car shop that used to be here. They don't take reservations, so stop by anytime for a fancy cocktail and a delicious plate of food.

The frozen Mexican martini is a shoo-in for the most popular drink at Holiday. Austin has gone crazy for this big, slushy, tequila-based beverage that is served in both small and large sizes. It's packed full of plenty of booze and has a briny olive finish. But the cocktail menu extends far beyond martinis with plenty of other options, like their lineup of "fancy cocktails," a daily selection of punch, and plenty of spirit-free non-alcoholic takes on craft cocktails.

While it might seem like a cock-tail bar at first sight, Holiday really is a full restaurant with plenty of bites, from snack-sized to large plates, that you'll want to try. Start with the cashew onion dip, which is tangy and rich and served with potato chips. The chopped kale salad is shockingly delicious, mixed with a generous amount of their yummy miso-tahini vinaigrette and big pieces of shaved Mahón cheese. And if you want something heartier, try their 44 Farms burger, or one of their customer-favorite pasta dishes.

This place is a holiday that you won't want to end.

5

PRETEND YOU'RE IN ITALY WITH NEAPOLITAN-STYLE PIES AT BUFALINA

If you're searching for some seriously delicious Neapolitan pizza in Austin, Texas, look no further than **BUFALINA**. This teeny east Cesar Chavez restaurant doesn't take reservations and only holds about 40 people, which means that there will be a dinner line on the weekends. If you show up and there's a wait in front of you, try to squeeze your way to the bar and order a glass of wine to sip while you wait for a table.

The star of the room is a large, white pizza oven imported from Naples, which heats upward of 900 degrees Fahrenheit, cooking each pie for 90 seconds or so. The result? A small pizza with a puffy, chewy crust, and a hot, cheesy center topped with fresh ingredients. These pizzas are no joke.

If you're a bit of a purist about your Neapolitan pizza styles and you want something classic, go with the Margherita. It's topped with a simple scattering of tomato, mozzarella, basil, and Parm, and it is perfection. And you can't go wrong with any of the fun variations they have with other toppings. I never get tired of the roasted mushroom pizza with caramelized onion.

The wine list at Bufalina is exactly what you would expect from a serious Italian pizzeria. The menu boasts an extensive list of Italian wines to be paired with your 12-inch Calabrese pizza. Order by the glass or by the bottle, and enjoy sips of wine with your decadent pizza feast.

6

SNEAK AWAY TO A SULTRY DATE NIGHT AT JUSTINE'S BRASSERIE

Moody, sultry, oh-so-sexy, **JUSTINE'S BRASSERIE** is a French kitchen that's tucked far enough away on Cesar Chavez to be a decent drive from the rush of the town. The only clue you have that you're in the right place is the flashing neon sign facing the sidewalk; the rest of the restaurant is hidden behind a tall wall of greenery. Reservations aren't accepted here for groups smaller than six, so you'll probably be spending some time at the bar while you wait for a table. Order a French 75 and a cheese board, and enjoy the jazz music and the sound of glasses clinking.

The kitchen stays open late, so if you're a night owl and are looking for a 10 p.m. dinner spot, plan on stopping here for a late-night bite. The French onion soup is a decadent starter, made with a homemade stock, sweet, caramelized onions, and covered in a thick layer of melted cheese. The classic French entrees are beautifully prepared. I love to order the *moules frites* paired with an elegant Chablis. The steamed mussels are served with a heap of delicate little fries, but you'll probably want to use some of the crusty French bread to soak up the buttery sauce. Another crowd favorite is the classic steak *frites;* enjoy the rosy pink ribeye and fries with your choice of sauce au poivre, tangy Roquefort sauce, or the *beurre maître d'.* The burger royale is among the best in town, served on a chewy ciabatta bun. There is no wrong choice here; Justine's is a restaurant that relies just as heavily on the seductive ambience as it does on the excellent food and drinks. Raise your glass of deep-red Bordeaux, breathe in the night air, and cozy up to your date.

THE EAST AUSTIN CRAWL

1. Start your day with a cappuccino at tiny-yet-mighty **FLEET COFFEE**, 2427 WEBBERVILLE RD., AUSTIN, (512) 212-7174, FLEETCOFFEE.COM

2. Cameras ready for brunch at the adorable **HILLSIDE FARMACY**, 1209 E. 11TH ST., AUSTIN, (512) 628-0168, HILLSIDEFARMACY.COM

3. Lunch at **UPTOWN SPORTS CLUB**, 1200 E. 6TH ST., AUSTIN, (512) 551-2013, UPTOWNSPORTS.CLUB

4. Try James Beard Award–winning tacos at **NIXTA TAQUERIA**, 2512 E. 12TH ST., AUSTIN, NIXTATAQUERIA.COM

5. Escape to Argentina at **BUENOS AIRES CAFÉ**, 1201 E. 6TH ST., AUSTIN, (512) 382-1189, BUENOSAIRESCAFE.COM

6. Eat locally, the Texas way, at **DAI DUE**, 2406 MANOR RD., AUSTIN, (512) 524-0688, DAIDUE.COM

7. Stop by Austin's favorite neighborhood restaurant, **BIRDIE'S**, 2944 E. 12TH ST. UNIT A, AUSTIN, BIRDIESAUSTIN.COM

8. Corn is the star at **SUERTE**, 1800 E. 6TH ST., AUSTIN, (512) 953-0092, SUERTEATX.COM

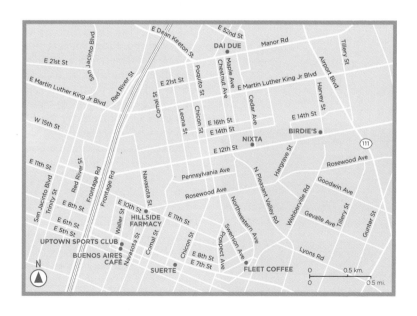

East Austin

Doing Our Best to Keep Austin Weird

OUR FOOD CRAWL CONTINUES JUST A FEW BLOCKS NORTH OF Cesar Chavez into east Austin. This is an all-encompassing title that I'm using to describe several small neighborhoods that all come together to create one big, food-dense region. (Insider tip: This area is PACKED with great boutique hotels and vacation rentals. If you're a foodie, rent a place to stay in east Austin and eat your heart out!)

East Austin has experienced more gentrification in the past decade than any other area of Austin. For a while, it was a low-income area of Austin. But proximity to downtown, among other reasons, has made it a trendy, expensive place to live with lots of mixed-use high-rise developments being built. With so many folks buying condos in east Austin, this is also a very popular place to open a restaurant.

You can find pretty much any type of food in east Austin. Sure, there are lots of amazing barbecue spots and farm-to-table restaurants, but there are also cool coffee shops, speakeasy-style cocktail bars, natural wine bars, and some of the best Mexican food in Austin.

There are some older, established Austin places still open, and I'll mention several of those. But there are also lots of fun, new, Insta-worthy hotspots that are worth a stop on your food crawl.

1

START YOUR DAY WITH A CAPPUCCINO AT TINY-YET-MIGHTY FLEET COFFEE

A perfect day begins with a perfect cup of coffee. **FLEET** is the best in east Austin; it takes pride in serving carefully prepared pour-overs, cappuccinos, and lattes. It's also the tiniest coffee shop in town. This small, triangular east Austin shop is just the right size for a walk-up counter and a few outdoor tables.

Lorenzo Perkins and Patrick Pierce opened this coffee shop after years of experience in Austin's best coffee shops. They've both won multiple awards at barista championships. They are, in a nutshell, the textbook example of "coffee nerds" and they chose to team up and open their own shop in a 364-square-foot corner of Webberville Road. The result? A perfectly comfortable, albeit tiny, place to stop by the coffee window and order a cappuccino to enjoy on the patio before starting your day.

The coffee is sourced from some of the world's most reputable coffee roasters, like Sweet Bloom Coffee Roasters and Junto Coffee, and Parlor Coffee Roasters from Brooklyn. This shop is an excellent place to buy your own bag of beans to brew at home. The staff is friendly and always generous with their time when I have questions about the various roasts that are available to purchase.

Fleet has recognizable bright blue cups, which make every one of their beautifully prepared coffee drinks completely photo-worthy.

Be sure to take a picture of that #dailycortado and post it to Instagram before heading off to brunch!

Coffee and a blueberry muffin? Nope! Austin is all about coffee and **breakfast tacos!** Most coffee shops here will have a few breakfast tacos on the menu. They're either made in the coffee shop, or catered in each morning from Tacodeli or Veracruz, two local taco shop chains.

2 CAMERAS READY FOR BRUNCH AT THE ADORABLE HILLSIDE FARMACY

The population surge in east Austin has forced restaurant developers to be creative in finding places to call home. The **HILLSIDE FARMACY** team decided to take an old, crumbling building that used to house Hillside Drugstore and restore and repurpose it into the most darling little cafe. This is an all-day eatery with a bright, vibrant feel and a combination of healthy and indulgent eats. The striped patio awning, vintage tile floor, and wallpapered walls instill an old-time soda fountain feel, but rest assured that the all-American menu, created by chef Sonya Coté, makes this adorable eatery more than just an Instagrammable spot. The food absolutely could stand on its own, even if this weren't such a darn cute little place full of so much ambience. The charcuterie, homemade snacks and sandwiches, and raw bar make this a tasty choice for any time of day. For first-timers, though, breakfast is the sweetest time to stop by.

Try the pancakes, which are made thick and fluffy and made with Mexican vanilla. Or for those who aren't interested in sugar for breakfast, the Big Brekki is a feast with two eggs, local fresh greens, blistered tomatoes, home fries, and your choice of bacon, sausage, or avocado. Whatever you order, enjoy the buzz of energy from dining at one of east Austin's most popular brunch spots.

Our next stop is inside another revitalized east Austin building.

3 LUNCH AT UPTOWN SPORTS CLUB

This one is fun! Austin has gone crazy for New Orleans-inspired restaurant **UPTOWN SPORTS CLUB**. It's partly because it was created by pitmaster Aaron Franklin (of Franklin Barbecue fame), and it's partly because he and his New Orleans native business partner James Moody restored this historic building on East 6th and Waller.

The 1890s building was completely falling apart and could have easily been one more demo/rebuild situation in Austin, but instead, the team took the space and meticulously revived it into one of the coolest spots to eat and drink in east Austin.

This is the perfect spot to be when you find yourself in east Austin and have a bit of free time to spare. Pop in, grab one of the barstools, and order a no-frills classic cocktail and a half-dozen East Coast oysters. Happy hour is a great opportunity to get some of their snacks and beverages at

a steal (try the smoked trout dip with Zapp's potato chips paired with a gin martini). The gumbo is incredible, made with chicken and sausage and served with warm white rice. And the po'boys are definitely the thing to order at Uptown Sports Club. There's a pretty big variety, but I love the fried green tomato sandwich the best (add bacon!) with lots of that yummy goddess ranch dressing on it.

Quite possibly the best part about Uptown is the menu of freezes. These are cold slushee desserts made with ice cream, so both kids and adults love them. They come in fun flavors like orange & cream or cherry jubilee, and you can make it a grown-up version by adding booze to it, if you'd like.

4 TRY JAMES BEARD AWARD–WINNING TACOS AT NIXTA TAQUERIA

These aren't your typical tacos! James Beard Award–winning chef Edgar Rico and Sara Mardanbigi are husband-wife co-owners of **NIXTA**, a tiny east Austin taqueria. From the beginning, they've been aiming to reinvent the expectations of Mexican-American cuisine . . . and WOW did they succeed!

The tortillas are made from nixtamalized heirloom Mexican corn. This means the staff at Nixta is working twice as hard as any other taco shop to make their tortillas, but you'll taste the result. The tortillas are soft and pliable, packed with a rich, nutty-grain flavor that only comes from heirloom corn that has been treated kindly.

The taco toppings aren't typical, either (in the best possible way!). They'll take a normal taco, like, say, a pork carnitas taco, and then mix it up by serving it with confit duck instead. Sometimes they'll make this crazy good "beet tartare," a very chef-y taco of roasted beets, bright avocado crema, *salsa macha*, horseradish, and micro greens.

Nixta somehow balances between being a casual spot where you can enjoy chips and queso and tacos with friends and being a destination-worthy restaurant that presents flavors and textures you've never tried before. If you're just going to visit one restaurant on your trip to Austin, Nixta would be an excellent and memorable choice.

Next up: another classic east Austin eatery, but this time with Argentine food!

5 ESCAPE TO ARGENTINA AT BUENOS AIRES CAFÉ

The front door of this buzzing Argentine cafe is constantly opening and closing with smiling customers who know and love Chef Reina and her daughter, Paola, who have been running this family business since the early 2000s. Reina, who was born and raised in Argentina, could only be asked to make her empanadas so many times before deciding to open her own little cafe. Opening a business as a female entrepreneur wasn't easy; Reina was turned down many times by potential lenders and landlords who didn't believe she would succeed. But perseverance paid off, and now Reina is the owner not only of this east side cafe, but also another location in west Austin.

The empanadas are a great place to start. Order the *carne picante*, full of spicy ground beef, green onions, raisins, green olives, and fresh herbs and spices, and enjoy that soft, flaky crust crumbling with every bite. **BUENOS AIRES CAFÉ** imports their oregano from Argentina to make the *provoleta*, a traditional Argentine charred provolone; Instagram that #cheesepull before scooping up the delicious melty dish onto crispy little pieces of bread.

Grilled meat is classic Argentine food; if you're only going to taste one thing from the grilled section of the menu, try the *parrillada*, which is a massive Argentine-style mixed grill of beef short ribs, chicken breast, and Chef Reina's house-made chorizo bratwurst.

Dessert is not to be missed here! The Dark and Spicy Crème Brûlée is an indulgent dark chocolate custard with spicy pasilla, cayenne peppers, and a few bright strawberries to counter the heat. Or try the lemon pie, made from Chef Reina's old family recipe of a graham cracker crust filled with lemon filling and Italian torched meringue.

After enjoying an Argentine feast, we're going to bring this food crawl back to Austin to enjoy something we do best: local Texas cuisine.

6 EAT LOCALLY, THE TEXAS WAY, AT DAI DUE

The restaurant name says it all: DAI DUE comes from the Latin phrase "from the two kingdoms of nature, choose food with care." James Beard Award–winning chef and author Jesse Griffiths is all about carefully sourcing local Texas meat and produce that has been grown fairly and safely, supporting the local ranchers and farmers, and, of course, creating a hearty and mouthwatering menu of choices for hungry customers.

Dai Due started as a supper club and a booth at the farmers' market, and gradually grew into its own brick and mortar. Everything here is as local as possible. Chef Jesse is passionate about using Texas game on his menu. He even goes so far as to organize hunting trips through his New School of Traditional Cookery. Customers can purchase a class to learn how to shoot, clean, and cook their own game, all while enjoying meals from the items covered in the class.

However, for many of us, we just want an exceptional dining experience, no hunting required. The beautiful east side restaurant is also a bakery and a butcher shop, so when you walk in, you'll see bakers kneading dough and you might even see a whole hog being wheeled on the ceiling track to the kitchen.

The menu is constantly evolving, so I can't offer too many suggestions and guarantee they'll be there when you dine. But since the bread is being made right in front of your eyes, grilled mesquite sourdough with Fresno chile–whipped lard is a delicious place to start. The meat is all cooked over

post oak. There's recognizable cuts, like a 48-hour aged wagyu NY strip, and there's also more unique Texas game on the menu, like a grilled half confit rabbit with mint marigold *soubise* and Aleppo pepper.

Dai Due has elevated the cuisine in Austin by not just sourcing from farm to table, but truly sourcing game that is native to Texas. Don't be scared off by chicken hearts or ground wild boar. This food is true Texas dining, and it's all delicious.

On your way out the door, stop by the butcher shop to purchase some grass-fed beef, free-roaming venison, or feral hog to cook at home. You'll have trouble finding another butcher shop in Austin that puts quite so much care into providing local and sustainably raised meat to their customers.

7 STOP BY AUSTIN'S FAVORITE NEIGHBORHOOD RESTAURANT, BIRDIE'S

The line might be wrapping around the building by the time you arrive at **BIRDIE'S**, but please don't let that deter you. This darling neighborhood wine bar and eatery is worth the wait!

The husband-wife owned restaurant was featured as the best restaurant of the year by *Food & Wine* magazine, and while that certainly helped with publicity, local Austinites knew this place was a gem from the moment it opened.

The concept is pretty simple: It's a fine-casual counter service restaurant that serves simple and upscale American cuisine. The menu changes every single day, which makes this a fun place to visit again and again.

While you're waiting in line, you can order a bottle of wine to start drinking. The staff here is so amazing—they'll walk you through the interesting wine list and help you find something you love, and then your wine will be brought to you in a little caddy of ice so that you can carry it with you as you travel through the line.

Once you step inside the (teeny) restaurant you'll order at the counter. (I like to get about 5 plates when I'm eating at Birdie's with a date.) And then you'll seat yourself and wait for food! The chef's counter is my very favorite place to sit because I love to watch the food being prepared in the micro kitchen.

Enjoy fresh veggie plates like roasted cauliflower and broccolini with *bagna cauda,* or their beef tartare with pecans, sonora, rosemary, and *carta di musica.* There are typically only 2 or 3 larger plates available, which feature a meat or seafood option like red snapper with Puy lentils, burgundy spinach, and potatoes. For dessert, be sure to try their yummy chocolate chip cookie.

One more stop on this east Austin food crawl. And yes, I'm aware that there are a lot of dinner options in this chapter . . . but that just speaks to the depth of high-quality restaurants in east Austin!

8 CORN IS THE STAR AT SUERTE

Sam Hellman-Mass, one of the cofounders of Odd Duck (see the Zilker chapter for more on Odd Duck) and chef Fermin Nuñez geeked out on all things corn before opening this award-winning restaurant. They traveled to Mexico, studied corn, figured out how to soak it and grind it and transform it into the most delectable corn tortillas you can possibly try, and then created a restaurant all about corn. Say hello to **SUERTE**.

The word means luck in Spanish, and you're going to feel all that good fortune that you stumbled into this restaurant. The adorable pink door is a preview of the lovely design aesthetic that you'll see inside. Almost everything in the restaurant was designed with textiles from Mexico and Texas, like the tequila bottle chandeliers, the Texas pecan wood used to make the tables, and the beautiful pink-striped fabric that lines the chairs.

This is a place to order a tequila- or mezcal-based cocktail, because

> "Making the masa and serving every tortilla warm from the first time it's cooked is the foundation of our cooking. The corn from Richardson Farms and Barton Springs Mill has a truly amazing flavor and Texas terroir."
>
> —*Sam Hellman-Mass, owner of Suerte*

they have a great selection of those liquors. The bartender will help you find something fun and new to try on the cocktail menu.

The food menu is meant to be shared, making this a great place to go on a double date. Order two or three plates per person and enjoy tasty ceviche, tacos, and tostadas, and slightly larger entrees. I adore Suerte because they manage to take ingredients that don't tend to have mouthwatering properties (the entire restaurant is based on a dry seed from the grass family, after all) and turn it into a delectable treat. Those tiny tortillas are the base of their famous *suadero* tacos, filled with confit wagyu brisket, black magic oil, avocado crudo, and onion and cilantro sprinkled on top. They're so completely satisfying that I've ordered them every time I dine here.

THE CLARKSVILLE CRAWL

1. Start your day with a French press at **MEDICI ROASTING**, 1101 W. LYNN ST., AUSTIN, (512) 524-5409, MEDICIROASTING.COM

2. Enjoy a posh lunch at **JOSEPHINE HOUSE**, 1601 WATERSTON AVE., AUSTIN, (512) 477-5584, JOSEPHINEOFAUSTIN.COM

3. Eat all day at **BETTER HALF COFFEE & COCKTAILS**, 406 WALSH ST., AUSTIN, (512) 645-0786, BETTERHALFBAR.COM

4. Raise your martini to happy hour at **CLARK'S OYSTER BAR**, 1200 W. 6TH ST., (512) 297-2525, CLARKSOYSTERBAR.COM

5. Snack on tapas at **ROSIE'S WINE BAR**, 1130 W. 6TH ST., AUSTIN, (512) 667-7187, ROSIESAUSTIN.COM/

6. Eat Austin's best soup dumplings at **LIN ASIAN BAR + DIM SUM**, 1203 W. 6TH ST., AUSTIN, (512) 474-5107, LINASIANBAR.COM

7. Dine under the stars at **BAR PEACHED**, 1315 W. 6TH ST., AUSTIN, (512) 992-0666, BARPEACHED.COM

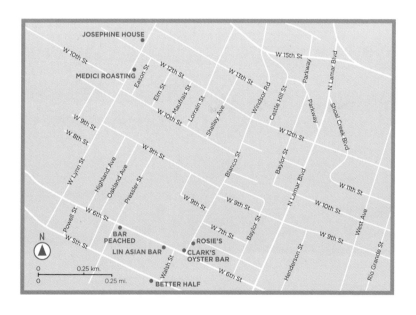

Clarksville

Stepping Back in Time

CLARKSVILLE IS A CHERISHED HISTORIC NEIGHBORHOOD; IT'S a little village of posh eateries, quaint coffee shops, and small houses from the early 1900s. It's the closest residential neighborhood to downtown Austin, so this is a fiercely competitive place to lock in real estate.

Clarksville dates back to 1871 and was named after its founder, freedman Charles Clark. It remains the oldest surviving freedom town west of the Mississippi. Sadly, Austin city policy pressured Black communities to move east in the early 20th century, and Clarksville became increasingly hostile toward the original founding members. The streets weren't fully paved until the 1970s, when Clarksville was declared an official historic district. Sums of money were provided to rehabilitate the houses and provide housing for various incomes, and fifth- or sixth-generation Clarksville residents still fight to keep the original houses and buildings of Clarksville standing.

Nowadays? Clarksville has become a HOT place to live. Lots of those bungalows have been torn down and new modern builds are towering in their place. But Clarksville still has a neighborhood feel, despite its proximity to downtown. Spending a day in Clarksville is a little bit like stepping back in history to a simpler version of Austin. From a cozy coffee shop in a renovated house, to a posh and polished oyster bar, Clarksville offers a fun day of strolling and eating for anyone who is lucky enough to visit.

1

START YOUR DAY WITH A FRENCH PRESS AT MEDICI ROASTING

Austin's coffee scene is booming, but once upon a time, there weren't many options except for gas station coffee and a national megachain (you know the one . . .). **MEDICI ROASTING** is "Austin's original specialty coffee shop." They started talking about tasting notes, high-quality beans, and French presses before it was even cool.

There are now multiple locations in Austin, but the original cafe started on quiet little West Lynn Street in Clarksville. Walk up the creaky wooden stairs and enter a cozy ambience: The air smells like freshly brewed coffee, and the sounds of clicking computer

keys and chattering conversation make you feel like you're walking into a big, happy living room. I love meeting up with a friend or spending my morning here working on my laptop.

Medici Roasting offers the coffee you would expect to see in a specialty coffee shop: several single-origin options and all of the typical espresso drinks. There's always a fresh batch of coffee ready, as well as a full lineup of espresso drinks.

This is one of the larger Austin coffee chains; if your Clarksville food crawl doesn't allow time to stop by, you might be able to venture into one of the other Medici Roasting locations around the city. Each location has its own mood, but they're all buzzy, high-energy, comfortable places to grab a caffeinated beverage and a breakfast taco to start your day.

Did you know that Whole Foods Market originated right here in Clarksville? Clarksville Natural Grocery, a small, independent grocery store in the Clarksville neighborhood of Austin, joined forces with another healthy grocery store in Austin and became the first Whole Foods Market in 1980.

2 ENJOY A POSH LUNCH AT JOSEPHINE HOUSE

If you've figured out how to resist a darling breakfast spot, tell me your secret. I'm a sucker for the whitewashed walls, the renovated 1920s houses, the sunny front porches, and the wicker chairs. I want it all.

JOSEPHINE HOUSE doesn't rely on good looks alone, though. Breakfast, lunch, happy hour, and dinner are all sure to please the hungry customer. The lemon ricotta pancakes are some of the fluffiest you'll find in the whole city. They're served with blackberries and cultured butter, and they are scrumptious! If you're stopping by for lunch or dinner, the charcuterie board is one of the tastiest and most Instagrammable starters. And I can't get enough of the Josephine House burger and *frites.* Those crispy little fries are irresistible!

3 EAT ALL DAY AT BETTER HALF COFFEE & COCKTAILS

The name has "coffee and cocktails" in it, but this all-day eatery is so much more! Sure, **BETTER HALF** serves incredible coffee, lattes, cappuccinos, and other specialty caffeinated beverages in the morning. And yes, they transition into a bar with cocktails, beer, and wine in the evenings. But they also have some of the best food in Austin, a gorgeous tree-shaded backyard patio, and an adjacent brewery that's run by the same folks but features its own food menu! There are clearly a lot of reasons why Better Half is included in this Clarksville food crawl.

If you stop by for breakfast and want to start with a hot beverage, they do the classics, like a whole-milk latte or a hot cup of black coffee, really well. But if you want something fancier, they often feature specialty lattes like a lavender latte, or a rosemary matcha. There are a few staple breakfast items on the daily menu (don't sleep on that breakfast sandwich—it looks simple, but the English muffin is made in-house and it's so good!), and the weekend brunch menu is more expansive if you're able to stop by on a Saturday or Sunday morning.

And since it's an all-day eatery, the menu evolves throughout the day to feature larger, heartier entrees in the evening hours. You'll find items

like a vermicelli salad with cold pulled smoked chicken, or a *mala*-spiced Taiwanese chicken sandwich. And the chips and queso are good at literally any time of day. But honestly, the classic Better Half Cheeseburger is my most ordered item here. It's a big, classic cheeseburger that's made with locally sourced beef. It's moderately priced (especially if you snag that happy hour deal!), and perfectly satisfying with a cocktail from the bar.

And like I mentioned, Clarksville is basically in downtown Austin. Which makes Better Half's parking situation so incredible. They not only have a parking lot in the front with a handful of spots, they also have a huge parking yard behind the property just off 4th Street. You're not going to find another bar, restaurant, or brewery so near downtown with this much parking!

4 RAISE YOUR MARTINI TO HAPPY HOUR AT CLARK'S OYSTER BAR

Oh, the charm! **CLARK'S OYSTER BAR** on West 6th Street is a buzzing and bustling bar with all of the textile treats for a design-lover's dream. The dining options are divided into three parts: a quaint bar area with round stools and a tall table for perching, a snug dining space with white tablecloths, and an outdoor patio with white and yellow striped umbrellas and cooling fans. This is a very popular place to enjoy ice-cold oysters and martinis in the summer. The entire restaurant has a beachy feel with nautical sea-green accents amid the bright-white tiles. It feels preppy and welcoming at the same time.

Enjoy your house-baked sourdough bread while you settle in and prepare to stay for a while; Clark's is made for lingering. Sip your champagne, slurp a fresh oyster, and . . . was that your imagination, or did you just feel a sea breeze from Cape Cod Bay? No, we're still in Austin. But the New England clam chowder will instantly transport you to a city that's not quite so landlocked.

Clark's is an oyster bar, but don't ignore the burger! It's a favorite in Austin. The Black Angus burger is pan-roasted and served with crunchy shoestring fries or a tangy slaw. Either option is delectable during a long and lazy lunch or happy hour.

Save room for one more drink at our next stop!

5

SNACK ON TAPAS AT ROSIE'S WINE BAR

Austin is fortunate to have many excellent wine bars. You can stroll through almost any part of town and find a cute place to stop in for an interesting glass of wine and a bite of food. **ROSIE'S WINE BAR** is a bit different because of (1) its size, and (2) its cute tapas menu.

The space is very small. The interior is basically a bar with a few barstools and some places to perch near the window. The outside patio is absolutely lovely on a nice Austin day, and it has all the European feels. It's a great spot to stop by in the late afternoon to share a bottle of wine with a friend. The rotating wine list has an emphasis on small producers and natural winemakers, but that's really the only constraint. There's a pretty big variety of wine available here, both by the glass and by the bottle.

If you're feeling snacky, the menu has some tapas-style plates, inspired by the cuisine of Spain and Portugal. Try the *jamón* and *manchego* toasts, which are the perfect finger food to enjoy with a bottle of Tempranillo. Rosie's offers plenty of Spanish cheeses to munch on, as well as seafood snacks like fried calamari with a squeeze of lemon, or *gambas al ajillo* (gulf shrimp with banana pepper). There are a few large-format entrees, too, like beef-stuffed *piquillo* peppers or steak *frites*. But I think that Rosie's really shines as a place to stop by for a bite and a leisurely glass of wine on their sidewalk cafe. Besides, you'll want to save room for dinner. Clarksville has a few really great options for an evening meal!

6

EAT AUSTIN'S BEST SOUP DUMPLINGS AT LIN ASIAN BAR + DIM SUM

If you've driven down West 6th Street, you've probably noticed a small house with hanging lanterns on the porch. It's called **LIN ASIAN BAR + DIM SUM**. Yes, it's eye-catching, and also yes—you should book a reservation here for dinner sometime soon!

If you remember reading about Qi in the Downtown Austin section, you already know quite a bit about Lin Asian Bar: It's a health-conscious Chinese restaurant that was started by chef Ling Qi Wu. Lin Asian Bar was actually her first Austin restaurant, opening back in 2019. It rose in popularity very quickly, hence the handful of additional restaurants that she's opened since then!

It's so much fun that Lin Asian Bar specializes in home cooking, because the restaurant itself is a renovated home. You'll enter the restaurant via the front porch, which is where you'll see all of those iconic hanging lanterns. The porch is my favorite place to dine on a warm evening, but the interior is cozy and quaint, and I love enjoying my dim sum in there, too. There's a private dining room available for rent—once when I was eating here, I saw the mayor of Austin walk in there to enjoy dinner with his group!

You could easily fill up on the dim sum alone. Be sure to try the scallion pancakes with curry dip, a variety of pot stickers, dumplings, and *sui mai,* and for SURE get an order of the famous Lin Soup Dumplings.

But save space for the noodles, rice, and entrees, too. I adore the seafood udon noodles and any of the fried rice options, but the sweet and rich volcano shrimp with honey pecan is my all-time favorite.

Lin Asian Bar's dim sum weekend brunch is an absolute treat—and Austinites know that! Brunch reservations will often be booked weeks in advance. But if you have your heart set on brunch and you can't get a reservation, or you're only in Austin on the weekdays, keep in mind that you can enjoy lots of the same dim sum offerings during their lunch and dinner services, too.

7 DINE UNDER THE STARS AT BAR PEACHED

Alfresco dining is a big thing in Austin, and we're lucky to have a lot of excellent outdoor patios that we can enjoy (mostly) year-round. **BAR PEACHED** on West 6th is one of those places, and it's also a phenomenal place to enjoy happy hour, cocktails with friends, or a fun and casual date night experience.

Chef Eric Silverstein calls this place a "bar-focused restaurant." It's like the more casual/chill younger sister to his original restaurant, Peached Tortilla (Brentwood chapter). But even though it has a laid back atmosphere, the fusion food is creative and a little bit fancy.

The main concept is Asian comfort food, but with a twist. The snacky plates are so much fun if you want to stop by for a happy hour on the outdoor patio under the Heritage Oak tree. Try the pork buns: pillowy soft steamed buns filled with Vietnamese braised pork belly, cucumber, green onions, and Chinese barbecue sauce. The spicy *gochu* pork fries are also so yummy, topped with kimchi and black sesame seeds, and the option to add a 14-minute egg.

For entrees, Bar Peached has a handful of fusion tacos. This means they're not like the Mexican street food tacos you might find at a local taqueria. Bar Peached starts with flour tortillas and fills these tacos with fun fillings to create unique tacos like a banh mi–inspired taco, a Texas barbecue brisket taco, and a spiced sweet potato taco with toasted peanuts and Kewpie mayo. And if you're really hungry, try the delicious *mapo* Bolognese, or the pesto udon noodles.

Draft cocktails here are breezy and easy, and many of them are available on the happy hour menu.

THE UNIVERSITY OF TEXAS CRAWL

1. Step back to the 1920s at **DIRTY MARTIN'S PLACE**, 2808 GUADALUPE ST.,
    AUSTIN, (512) 477-3173, DIRTYMARTINS.COM

2. Visit **SCHOLZ GARTEN**, Austin's oldest restaurant, 1607 SAN JACINTO BLVD.,
    AUSTIN, (512) 474-1958, SCHOLZGARTEN.COM

3. Get a taste of Ethiopia at **ASTER'S**, 2804 N. INTERSTATE HWY. 35, AUSTIN,
    (512) 469-5966, ASTERSETHIOPIANKITCHEN.COM

4. Cozy up with French food and beer at **HOPFIELDS**, 3110 GUADALUPE ST.
    STE. #400, AUSTIN, (512) 537-0467, HOPFIELDSAUSTIN.COM

5. Marvel at the modern Southern food at **OLAMAIE**, 2938 GUADALUPE ST.,
    AUSTIN, (512) 476-5955, ELPATIOAUSTIN.COM

6. Visit **CROWN & ANCHOR PUB**, Austin's best watering hole, 2911 SAN
    JACINTO BLVD., AUSTIN, (512) 322-9168, CROWNANDANCHORPUB.COM

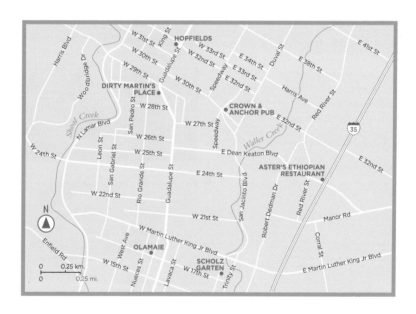

University of Texas

Austin Eats for Dorm-Dwellers

IF YOU FALL UNDER THE DEMOGRAPHIC OF BROKE 19-YEAR-OLD college student who will never say no to an all-you-can-eat buffet, this chapter is for you. Say hello to Austin's most student-friendly foodie area: University of Texas.

For this chapter, we're going to be covering eateries that are near UT, but not necessarily on campus: West Campus, Guadalupe, and one of my favorite areas: The Drag.

Located on the western border of the University of Texas at Austin campus, The Drag is a 10-block stretch of Guadalupe Street that caters to UT students. This is where you can find dive bars, campus bookstores, funky fashion stores, and (most importantly for this book) delicious eats.

Walking along The Drag is a great way to spend a day food crawling through Austin, because there are a few good coffee shops and some great local breakfast and lunch spots. And while "cheap eats" is often on the forefront of any college student's mind, I've included a few upscale eateries in this chapter, too. After all, you need some good suggestions on hand for when your parents offer to take you out to eat!

I adore eating near campus for a couple of reasons. First, it brings me back to my days at the University of Texas. Eating out is slightly more fun now that I can afford both the drink and the chips with my sandwich without worrying about having any grocery money left. Secondly, since UT is in central Austin, just north of downtown, that means some of the restaurants here have been around since the early 1900s.

Take Dirty Martin's Place, for instance. Walk into this little burger shack, and you'll see photos on the wall of what Austin looked like in 1930. Dirty Martin's is still in the original location it held back then, although what's around it has completely changed. The restaurant used to be in what was very far north Austin, but as Austin has grown and grown, it's now considered central.

Get ready to eat and drink your way through some of UT Austin's favorite restaurants from the past 100 years.

1

STEP BACK TO THE 1920S AT DIRTY MARTIN'S PLACE

No, the name doesn't mean this place is in need of a good scrub. **DIRTY MARTIN'S PLACE** originally had dirt floors when it opened as an eight-stool drive-in back in 1926. The restaurant's interior was paved in 1951, and some things have changed, but the important stuff remains: They still make the same 100 percent Angus beef burgers and onion rings that they did back in 1926.

As the cost of living increases in Austin, many old institutions have closed their doors. Dirty Martin's Place stays relevant in all of the important ways, like serving really good burgers and fries, acquiring a liquor license to cater to the pre-game UT football fans, all while still keeping their old-school charm.

Be sure to try the hand-cut onion rings and fries, prepared fresh every day. This is a family-friendly place where everyone, young and old, will enjoy classic diner food like fried pickles, bacon cheeseburgers, and vanilla malts.

The walls are adorned with framed memorabilia, like the original menu from Dirty Martin's Place. The price of a hamburger in 1926? Twenty-five cents!

Next up: another institution that's recognized as the oldest restaurant in Austin.

> "Many of our customers have been coming to Dirty's since the 1930s and 1940s. It is an Austin and University of Texas tradition to come to Dirty Martin's. We are an Austin institution. We have many longtime employees who know the customers like they are family. We treat our employees like family."
>
> —Daniel Young, GM of Dirty Martin's Place

2

VISIT SCHOLZ GARTEN, AUSTIN'S OLDEST RESTAURANT

Prost! **SCHOLZ GARTEN** is a German restaurant near University of Texas that opened in 1866 when August Scholz, a German immigrant and Civil War veteran, paid $2,400 for the building. It started as a popular place for the German population in Austin, but in more recent years, it has become the go-to spot for pregaming before a Longhorn football game.

The outdoor garden will be absolutely packed on game days! Folks show up in burnt orange and order German bratwurst and house-made sauerkraut and big pitchers of German lager. There's often live music playing on the outdoor stage, and a lot of energy in the air.

Of course, you can stop by on any day, regardless of the college football schedule or your university affiliation. Scholz's is a large restaurant, so it's popular for Oktoberfest, outdoor concerts, and game day showings on the big screen. But it's also a fun spot to stop by and order a Reuben sandwich with haus-made corned beef, a pan-fried wiener schnitzel, or just a big Bavarian pretzel with a pint of German beer.

3

GET A TASTE OF ETHIOPIA AT ASTER'S

There are certain buildings in Austin that everyone knows. The UT Tower. The Capitol. The Jo's Coffee "I Love You So Much" building. And then . . . there's this one. Often referred to as the "blue-building-on-the-side-of-I-35," **ASTER'S ETHIOPIAN RESTAURANT** is a family-owned establishment that's beloved by UT students, former and present.

You'll start by choosing your main meat or vegetarian entree. *Doro wott* is a great place to start—it's Ethiopia's national dish of chicken that's been slowly simmered in a flavorful *berbere* sauce and Ethiopian spices like cardamom, garlic, cumin, and fenugreek. Each main dish is served with a

variety of vegetarian side dishes, like rich and flavorful lentils and potatoes. No need to use a fork—you'll be given plenty of *injera* flatbread. It's a
thin, spongy bread that you can use to scoop up all the flavorful meats and
sauces. It has a bit of a vinegar-y taste, and the acid mixes well with the
richness in the hearty stews.

If the restaurant looks small from the outside, it's because . . . it is! But
there's an adjacent sunroom to accommodate the lunch crowd. UT students love filling up on the all-you-can-eat lunch buffet, and Austinites of
all ages adore this place for a hearty dinner or a take-out meal to enjoy at
home on a cold evening.

If you're ready for a craft beer or a cocktail, next up on our University of
Texas food crawl is an unfussy French gastropub.

4

COZY UP WITH FRENCH FOOD AND BEER AT HOPFIELDS

Dark and cozy are the first two words that come to mind to describe this sweet little French spot that was opened in 2011 by beer lover Bay Anthon. Hopfields serves approachable and uncomplicated French food, which one would typically expect to be paired with wine. But they went a little Austin on us (keeping things weird, for those of you who forgot the slogan . . .) and decided to specialize in craft beer instead of wine. That is one of the many things that make **HOPFIELDS** a unique spot to stop on your day of eating through Austin. And no worries if you're not a beer drinker—Hopfields also has an excellent selection of wine, as well as craft cocktails.

This is a fun place to visit solo, on a date, or with a group. Dining alone? Snag a seat at the small counter near the front door. You'll have a first-row seat to the rotating tap bar, and you can bug the bartender with all of your beer questions as you dive into that hearty Pascal Burger, a decadent patty topped with Camembert, cornichons, whole-grain mustard, and caramelized onions on a fluffy brioche bun. It's served with their famous *frites* and house-made aioli. If you're here on a date, lucky you! This is a romantic place because there are several nooks and crannies where you can enjoy a

quiet meal and conversation. There's also a back room available to rent for large groups who love to enjoy French food and craft beer.

I like to start my meal with their dreamy poutine. The *frites* are sturdy with a little bit of crisp, and they're topped with decadent brown gravy and salty cheese cruds. The *moules frites* are among the best in Austin, presented in a very generous serving size of PEI mussels in that yummy white wine and garlicky butter sauce and a huge heap of fries.

Ok, we can't food crawl through University of Texas without mentioning one of the highest-regarded restaurants in Austin. When it comes time to splurge on a nice dinner out, be sure to bookmark this next one.

5 MARVEL AT THE MODERN SOUTHERN FOOD AT OLAMAIE

OLAMAIE is an upscale Southern restaurant with multiple James Beard Award nominations and semifinalist awards, and the first thing you need to know about this place is that you cannot leave without tasting the off-the-menu biscuits.

No matter if you've made reservations for Sunday brunch, a formal weekend date night, or just a regular Tuesday night dinner, the biscuits must be ordered. They're soft, buttery pillows of dough that hardly need any toppings, but the honey butter served on the side doesn't hurt.

The unassuming white bungalow that houses Olamaie has been many different concepts in its years, but step inside the newly designed space and you'll experience an air of celebration. This is no dingy, dusty, Southern restaurant; Olamaie's interior bright white walls, taupe accents, and tufted bench seats give off a feeling of sophistication. Enter the restaurant by walking through a winding porch and a charming sitting area. Waiting for a table? Treat yourself to one of their beautiful cocktails or a homemade soda to pass the time.

Although the concept is elevated Southern cuisine, don't expect to recognize the menu items as typical Southern food.

The menu shifts almost daily because all of the ingredients are local, sourced within 200 miles of Austin. When I see them on the menu, I love to order the Hopi Blue Corn Hushpuppies. They're not your typical hush puppies! Made with hopi blue cornmeal from local Barton Springs Mill, these delicate bites are a bright, almost purple color on the inside, and served with caramelized onion dip and trout roe. The Blackened Dayboat Fish will change seasonally, but it's typically served with a flavorful blue crab sauce and a delicate serving of classic Carolina Gold rice. This restaurant is about the entire experience, from the friendly hospitality to the modern and memorable interior to (of course!) the menu of elevated Southern food. So plan on enjoying pre-dinner drinks, appetizers (hint: BISCUITS!), several dishes to share, and a lovely Southern dessert of zucchini bread with honeycomb ice cream.

If you're up for one more stop, this next casual pub near UT is a must-visit.

6

VISIT CROWN & ANCHOR PUB, AUSTIN'S BEST WATERING HOLE

We're going to wrap up this day of eating near University of Texas with a late-night pint at **CROWN & ANCHOR PUB**, one of Austin's best (and oldest!) watering holes near UT campus. It's been here since 1987, and it's open every day of the week, 365 days of the year. So if you're a student who's stuck on campus during a holiday, this is the place to go for a burger and a game of darts.

The same regulars have been going here since they were in college in the 80s, and the same owner, Derven Rodgers, is still behind the bar filling pint glasses.

The food isn't fancy, but you can order from a selection of hearty burgers, fries, and nachos. Enjoy them on the outdoor street-facing patio, or find a cozy table inside where you can watch the game or play a game of pool. Thirsty? The beer selection has about 30 taps, most of them local options, plus about 30 bottles and cans.

You won't find any fancy craft cocktails, tasting menus, or white tablecloths here. What you will find, though, is a covered dog-friendly patio, a smiling bartender, and a room full of welcoming Austinites who have been enjoying this institution since 1987.

THE HYDE PARK CRAWL

1. Let's start with some coffee at **FIRST LIGHT BOOK SHOP**, shall we?
   4300 SPEEDWAY UNIT 104, AUSTIN, (512) 996-1516, FIRSTLIGHTAUSTIN.COM

2. Get your green juice fix at **JUICELAND**, 4500 DUVAL ST., AUSTIN,
   (512) 380-9046, JUICELAND.COM

3. Nosh on homemade pies and pastries at **QUACK'S 43RD STREET
   BAKERY**, 411 E. 43RD ST., AUSTIN, (512) 453-3399, QUACKSBAKERY.COM

4. Stop by the cutest all-day Italian spot at **UNCLE NICKY'S**, 4222 DUVAL ST.,
   AUSTIN, (512) 318-2877, UNCLENICKYS.COM

5. Take a cheese-tasting class at **ANTONELLI'S CHEESE SHOP**, 4220 DUVAL ST.,
   AUSTIN, (512) 531-9610, ANTONELLISCHEESE.COM

6. Bon appétit at **BUREAU DE POSTE**, 4300 SPEEDWAY STE. 100, AUSTIN,
   (512) 375-3320, BUREAUDEPOSTEATX.COM

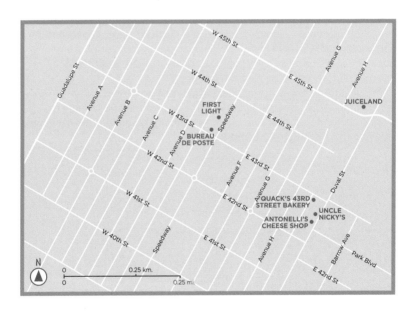

Hyde Park

Austin's First Suburb

IF YOU STROLL THROUGH HYDE PARK TODAY, YOU'LL STILL SEE glimpses of its history: an affluent suburb for Austin's upper class. The neighborhood was developed in the late 1800s as a "street car neighborhood," which basically means Hyde Park was considered to be WAY OUT in the suburbs. (Which is hilarious, because Austin's suburbs spread far and wide now and Hyde Park is practically considered downtown!). Although there are now plenty of renovated bungalows and modern duplexes, you can still see many of those original Queen Anne–style mansions and large, grassy estates lining the streets.

One of the coolest things to do in Hyde Park (besides eat your way through it!) is to stop by the Elisabet Ney Museum. It's a completely free experience where visitors can stop by the former art studio (aka mansion) of sculptor Elisabet Ney and see where she lived and worked. She's famous for those life-size statues of Sam Houston and Stephen F. Austin, which were created for the Texas State Capitol and are now currently displayed in the US Capitol in Washington, DC.

With University of Texas just below it, and North Loop on its north border, Hyde Park is a central Austin neighborhood that offers a lovely, tree-shaded, suburban oasis for families in Austin. This a fun place to take a leisurely stroll or bike ride. And with more and more fantastic restaurants opening in Hyde Park, it's becoming quite the foodie destination, too!

In fact, I'm going to say that this Hyde Park chapter is probably one of the most approachable chapters in the book. You really could spend just one day here and eat at every single place I mention in this chapter. You can break up the day with a visit to the Elisabet Ney Museum, take a bike ride, and visit the adorable local book shop before continuing on to your next meal.

I'm so excited to walk you through some of the best foodie finds in the neighborhood.

1

LET'S START WITH SOME COFFEE AT FIRST LIGHT BOOK SHOP, SHALL WE?

Coffee and books . . . it's hard to think of a better combo. And **FIRST LIGHT BOOK SHOP** is the coziest little spot to enjoy both of them. This independent bookstore on Speedway was originally a post office, which was meticulously renovated into the bright and airy bookstore, coffee shop, and wine bar that you can visit today.

There's a walk-up window at the front of the building, so you could easily grab a cup of coffee and a breakfast taco and take it to-go. But I highly recommend you walk inside and browse the shelves. There's a lovely selection of curated books, hand selected by First Light's book-loving owners. One of my favorite parts about visiting small, local book shops is finding the staff recommendation cards that are tucked among the books. I love finding something new and bringing it home as a souvenir of my travels.

The cafe offers espresso, pastries, and other light breakfast and lunch items. You'll also find grab-and-go sandwiches, potato chips, crudités with hummus, and a "lunchable" plate with cheese and salami and crackers available for purchase. Of course, you can't go wrong with an iced latte that you can sip while you browse the books.

If you're hoping for a casual glass of wine and a snack, First Light is wonderful in the afternoon and evening, too. They often host events, like conversations with notable authors, cultural discussions, and a weekly story time for little ones in the children's corner. They even host a monthly book club, which is free and open to the public.

Enjoy your coffee and pastries, purchase a book or two, and when you're ready, mosey over to our next stop.

2 GET YOUR GREEN JUICE FIX AT JUICELAND

Austin is fortunate to be home of many excellent juice companies, but JUICELAND has been the fastest growing among them. In fact, it's growing so fast, you can now find Juiceland locations all over Texas, including multiple locations in Austin, Dallas, and Houston. (Psst: there's a Juiceland at the Austin airport in case you need a delicious smoothie when your flights lands!) What makes this juice brand so great? Probably the "Austin-ness" about it. It was started in 2001 by Matt Shook in a small cave-like nook on Barton Springs. (That location is still open, and definitely worth checking out!)

The company is built on the idea of having fun, and there's nothing more Austin-y than that! They also care about health and acceptance and gratitude and mindfulness . . . basically all of the hippy-dippy things that are

easy to poke fun at, but are actually some of the most important components of a meaningful life. Juiceland takes great pride in their cold-pressed juices, tasty smoothies, shots, superfood lattes, and vegan food.

The drink names are pretty funny, because why use a normal smoothie name when you can use a way AWESOME name instead? The Wundershowzen with almond milk, banana, spinach, hemp protein, and peanut butter is one of their bestsellers, as is the Percolator, a tasty chocolate banana drink with caffeine from cold-brew coffee and cacao. Try the Recovery Punch if you need the ultimate hydration. It's made with watermelon juice, coconut water, and sea salt. All of the fresh juices are raw and made to order, or you can grab a bottle of cold-pressed juice if you're in a hurry and want something on the run.

And don't worry, I'm not going to get too healthy on you . . . our next stop is an old-school Austin bakery where you can get cinnamon rolls, cupcakes, and whole pies.

3

NOSH ON HOMEMADE PIES AND PASTRIES AT QUACK'S 43RD STREET BAKERY

A longtime institution in Austin, Quack's is the reincarnation of "Captain Quackenbush's Intergalactic Dessert Company and Espresso Cafe." That name is quite the mouthful! Thankfully, it was shortened to **QUACK'S 43RD STREET BAKERY** when the bakery moved to its current location in Hyde Park.

This is a neighborhood spot. Families with young students bike here on Saturday mornings, UT students walk in to get a coffee and a blueberry muffin before starting their days, and tourists are constantly walking in to try a slice of Quack's apple cinnamon pie.

The vibes are unpretentious and casual. Anyone is welcome, so you're just as likely to see a group of moms pushing strollers in as you are to see a couple of UT students meeting up for a study session.

The pastry case is full of all sorts of yummy treats, and it's hard to decide what to try! The apple cinnamon pie is widely regarded as one of the best in Austin. The crust has visible layers of butter and flour, and the overflowing pie is covered in a thick, crumbly layer of butter, sugar, and spices. If it's wrong to eat the crumb topping off a pie, I don't want to be right. Grab a slice at the bakery or order a whole pie for a special occasion.

The peanut butter fudge cake is layered with thick, fluffy frosting and covered in a dense chocolate ganache. This cake is dreamy!

The Ginger Krinkle cookie is packed with spicy ginger and covered with a thick sprinkle of sugar. If ginger is your thing, you have to try this cookie.

Indulge, my friend! Then, when you're ready for something a bit more substantial, head on over to Uncle Nicky's.

4

STOP BY THE CUTEST ALL-DAY ITALIAN SPOT AT UNCLE NICKY'S

UNCLE NICKY'S is an easy-breezy all-day spot that mimics the cafe culture of northern Italy. It is the brainchild of the team behind Via 313, Juniper, and Nickel City, so it has a phenomenal hospitality team backing it. The concept is a casual, all-day Italian cafe. If you've ever been to Milan and stopped by a cafe for an espresso in the morning, you'll recognize the familiar energy. Much of the cafe is occupied by bar-height tables with no chairs, made for perching for a quick espresso and a vanilla cruller while you scan the news in the morning, or a quick meal of a classic *pane tostato* in the afternoon.

Guests are welcome to stay for a while and leisure over happy

hour drinks, aperitivo, or maybe a full meal of salad (try the kale e *tartufo*—so delicious!) and a big plate of homemade spaghetti and pork meatballs.

But where Uncle Nicky's really shines is in the casual, no-frills, "stop-in-for-a-bite" type of moments. If you have a few minutes to spare and you feel that you could use a little pick-me-up, stop in! Order a spritz, a crispy piadina (a savory Italian flatbread, folded over warm, melty fillings like cheese and red sauce—it looks very similar to a quesadilla!), and an order of olive oil sardines and Ritz crackers. Enjoy a few minutes of turning your brain off and escaping from whatever is going on in your life, and enjoy the cafe music, the people around you, and the delicious food. Sip your drink, chat with a friend, scroll through your phone, and then you're on your way.

It's a simple, easy, every day sort of place, and Uncle Nicky's is a wonderful place to visit in Hyde Park.

5

TAKE A CHEESE-TASTING CLASS AT ANTONELLI'S CHEESE SHOP

Welcome to the sweetest little place to browse and taste and shop for cheese in Austin. You can't walk into this shop and not smile from ear to ear.

Here's the backstory on **ANTONELLI'S CHEESE**. John and Kendall Antonelli got married, and on their honeymoon, John said "I'd like to open a cheese shop." Swoon. Most romantic conversation ever! Two years later, Antonelli's Cheese Shop opened in Hyde Park, where guests can walk in and talk to knowledgeable cheese mongers and taste the latest and greatest in the cheese world.

Whether you're hosting a fancy dinner party, or just gathering to drink wine with some girlfriends on a weeknight, Antonelli's will be able to help you find the perfect cheese and accompaniments to pair with your drinks and satisfy your palate.

The small Hyde Park store is a bounty of artisanal foodie treats like honeycomb, seasonal jam, locally made chocolate bars, and fresh baguettes. There's a beautiful wine selection lining the wall. You can walk into this store empty-handed and come back out with everything you need to host an impressive backyard wine and cheese night.

John and Kendall Antonelli realized that lots of people want to learn more about cheese, so they opened their Cheese House across the street from the Cheese Shop. Curious customers can sign up for classes like "Cheese 101: The 7 Styles of Cheese" or "Holiday Pairings: How to Celebrate with Cheese!" These classes are a great date-night idea.

Another great date-night idea? French food, which is where we're heading for dinner!

6 BON APPÉTIT AT BUREAU DE POSTE

Remember First Light Book Shop, that post office turned bookstore that I mentioned at the beginning of this chapter? Well, part of the old post office was turned into the bookstore, but the other half of that post office was renovated into the most adorable specialty grocery store with a French restaurant outpost.

BUREAU DE POSTE is a cozy little spot that serves modern takes on French cuisine. Since it's an outpost within Tiny Grocer, it's a small space with a few barstools, some four-top tables, and then a larger outdoor patio.

The concept came from chef Jo Chan, who is notable in Austin for her previous work at Eberly on South Lamar, but you might recognize the name from her appearance in Top Chef.

The menu that she created at Bureau de Poste covers all of the French classics: escargot, French onion soup, *moules et frites,* and a beautiful burger royale. Every evening features different *plats du jour,* a rotating specialty item that's available that night and that night only. As I write this, the Tuesday plat du jour is Lobster

Frites, and it's phenomenal. That is, if you enjoy a half lobster that's been pan seared, and then basted with white wine and herb butter, and served with a hefty portion of crisp little *frites* and a dollop of aioli on the side.

The wine menu is lovely. There's a diverse selection on the menu, but since Bureau de Poste is located within a specialty grocery store, your server can select any bottle of wine that's sold onsite for you to enjoy with your meal.

Still hungry for dessert? Be sure to get that classic vanilla crème brûlée, which you can watch being torched in the open prep station just before it's brought to your table, all caramelized on top and perfectly creamy underneath.

WHAT DO AUSTIN CHEFS DO ON THEIR NIGHTS OFF?

"Most of my Austin friends are in the service industry, so I love visiting them when I'm off. Whether it's a pizza at Bufalina, sushi at Fukumoto, or a glass of wine at Neighborhood Vintner, it's wonderful to be on the receiving end of hospitality. Then they come to visit me and I can return the favor!"

—Chef Jo Chan,
Bureau de Poste

THE NORTH LOOP CRAWL

1. Brunch on farm-to-table fare at **FOREIGN & DOMESTIC**, 306 E. 53RD ST., AUSTIN, (512) 459-1010, FNDAUSTIN.COM

2. Drink coffee 24/7 at **EPOCH COFFEE**, 221 W. NORTH LOOP BLVD., AUSTIN, (512) 454-3762, EPOCHCOFFEE.COM

3. Chow down on burgers, latkes, and burritos at **JEWBOY BURGERS**, 5111 AIRPORT BLVD., AUSTIN, (512) 291-3358, JEWBOYBURGERS.COM

4. Snack on homestyle Japanese food at **KOMÉ**, 5301 AIRPORT BLVD. #100, AUSTIN, (512) 712-5700, KOME-AUSTIN.COM

5. Eat dinner at Austin's oldest seafood counter, **QUALITY SEAFOOD MARKET**, 5621 AIRPORT BLVD., AUSTIN, (512) 452-3820, QUALITYSEAFOODMARKET.COM

6. Order a craft cocktail at **DRINKWELL**, 207 E. 53RD ST., AUSTIN, (512) 614-6683, DRINKWELLAUSTIN.COM

7. Hang out with the locals at **WORKHORSE BAR**, 100 E. NORTH LOOP #B, AUSTIN, (512) 553-6756, THEWHITEHORSEAUSTIN.COM

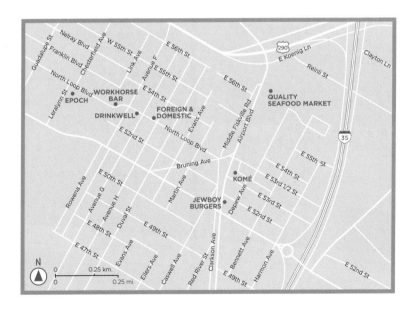

North Loop

The South Congress of North Austin

THE NORTH LOOP NEIGHBORHOOD IS CURRENTLY EXPERIENCING what South Congress went through several decades ago: It's cool. Like, really really cool. However, unlike SoCo, which has an increasing number of national brand-name stores buying out the old independent shops, North Loop is still mostly full of independent stores and restaurants, at least for the time being.

Welcome to the north Austin neighborhood where everyone wants to be. It's a little less expensive than its southern neighbor Hyde Park, and it's slightly more "Austin-y" than its eastern neighbor Mueller. Vintage clothing stores, weird car washes, hybrid coffee shop/bars, and lots of neighborhood restaurants provide just enough of the fun factor to turn a quiet residential neighborhood into one of the hottest places to buy a home in Austin.

While you make your way through this food crawl, embrace the rustic factor of these restaurants. This is not a sleek and polished neighborhood, like downtown Austin or South Congress. North Loop is a little rough around the edges, and we like it that way.

1

BRUNCH ON FARM-TO-TABLE FARE AT FOREIGN & DOMESTIC

You know those places you walk into and immediately get the warm fuzzies because you know everything about it is special? That's **FOREIGN & DOMESTIC**. This place was one of the first farm-to-table restaurants in Austin. They offer comforting food and warm hospitality in their teeny tiny north Austin space. How small is it? Well, the corner kitchen takes up a good ⅓ of the interior space, and an L-shaped counter wraps around the kitchen so dining customers can watch what's being prepared. The small amount of floor space that's left is full of little two- and four-top tables that can be pushed together to accommodate a group.

Chefs Sarah Heard and Nathan Lemley both come from small Texas towns, and they appreciate the food that Texas is able to provide. They source it carefully, making sure that the meat they serve is raised humanely, the crops are grown without yucky pesticides, and it's all coming from nearby, family-owned farms. From there, they use their expert touch to create gorgeous, shareable (or not!) plates that reflect the seasons. Dinner is offered five nights of the week, and a slow and lazy weekend brunch is served every Sunday morning.

The fried chicken biscuit is somewhat famous for being featured on Food Network's *Diners, Drive-ins, and Dives* with Guy Fieri, and if you're feeling famished, it's for you: fried chicken thigh and a sunny-side egg are placed on a warm biscuit, covered in red-eye gravy, and served with lemon confit. Another crowd favorite is the 44 Farms Steak and Eggs. 44 Farms is a family-owned cattle farm about 75 miles northeast of Austin. Since Foreign & Domestic starts with high-quality beef, you know your breakfast is going to be insanely delicious.

I once celebrated a birthday here with my husband. We sat at the counter, drank cocktails, and watched our delicious feast being prepared. It remains one of my favorite birthday meals to this day! Whether you stop by for dinner, brunch, or their daily happy hour, Foreign & Domestic will win you over.

Keep crawling for another fun North Loop breakfast spot.

2 DRINK COFFEE 24/7 AT EPOCH COFFEE

There are quite a variety of coffee shops in Austin. If you venture downtown you'll find the sleek, modern ones with glass walls and tiny chairs and tables for sipping a quick shot of espresso before heading on your way. But up here in the North Loop neighborhood, things are a bit slower and funkier. EPOCH COFFEE is a local favorite with multiple locations in Austin, and the North Loop spot is one of the best.

Established in 2006, Epoch is beloved for its well-worn antique furniture, indie music playing on the speakers, and all-around cozy and welcoming aesthetic. This is the coffee house where you're most likely to find a highly caffeinated college student pulling an all-nighter to pound out a term paper hours before it's due. Why? Epoch Coffee's North Loop location is open 24 hours a day. Yep! You can stop by for a chai tea at 2 p.m. or you can order a double espresso at 2 a.m. And there will be people working, chatting, or just hanging out at both times.

The coffee shop menu is fairly simple: coffee, tea, and espresso, with special seasonal lattes and house-made syrups to round things out. There are some pastries on the counter which are served on mismatched vintage plateware.

When your next creative burst strikes at 11 p.m. and you need a place to get away from the roommates and go work for the next 6 hours, head to Epoch. Who knows how many book manuscripts, business plans, and Literature 101 papers have been written within these walls?

3

CHOW DOWN ON BURGERS, LATKES, AND BURRITOS AT JEWBOY BURGERS

Mo Pittle is a guy who drew inspiration from his Reform Jewish upbringing and paired it with his US/Mexico border culture background to open a burger restaurant that we are, quite frankly, absolutely obsessed with. These might be the best burgers you've ever tried. No, they're not the fancy, expensive, chef-y burgers at a fine dining farm-to-table restaurant. These are classic, craveable, casual cheeseburgers that have developed a cult following. Take one bite, and you'll see why so many people call **JEWBOY** the best burgers in Austin.

This is a counter service restaurant, with the option to place your order ahead online. If it's your first time dining here, start with the Yenta burger. It's a ⅓ pound all-beef patty that's cooked on a super hot grill, so it gets that yummy, crispy char on the outside. They add some cheese and steam it until it's all ooey-gooey melty, and it's served on a soft potato bun with lettuce, pickles, and onion. And this next part seems weird, but just go with it: They add a latke to the burger. You can choose between a classic onion and garlic latke, or a green chile and cheddar latke. They're both deep-fried to golden perfection, and they make this burger absolutely unbeatable.

If you need further proof that Austin is obsessed with this restaurant, just look at all the burritos on the menu. I mean . . . what? We are 100 percent NOT a burrito town. Austin is all about tacos. Yet folks come back again and again for those massive burritos filled with marinated ribeye, refried beans, house-made guacamole, and yes, latkes. Latkes inside a burrito. Why not?

This isn't really a place to go halvsies. Get a giant burger, or burrito and order some tots with a side of chili con queso . . . and maybe some onion rings while you're at it. Go all out, because these burgers are worth it.

4

SNACK ON HOMESTYLE JAPANESE FOOD AT KOMÉ

This is a casual, family-style variance to all of the trendy sushi places we see so often. KOMÉ has a reasonable price point and serves Japanese comfort food, so it's no surprise that guests visit this place again, and again, and again. Husband-wife team Také and Kayo Asazu wanted to create an atmosphere that was almost like walking into someone's home to eat, so they opened Komé. Rather than offering typical Japanese restaurant food, they created a menu that focuses on Japanese homestyle cooking. This place serves excellent Japanese food like sushi, sashimi, bento boxes, and ramen, but rather than having a strictly authentic Japanese feel, the food also comes with little splashes of Austin and New Orleans, cities where the owners have lived. Komé is so popular, it outgrew the original location and moved into a larger building down the street.

When you walk in, you'll be greeted by the entire staff saying "irrashaimasé!" which means "welcome!" in Japanese. It should put a smile on your face. The counter is a fun place to sit if you're dining solo, because you can chat with your server and watch the sushi chefs preparing your meal.

If you're stopping by for lunch, try one of the Komé bento lunches. You'll be able to try miso soup, *kara-agé, agé-dashi* tofu, *harusame* noodle salad, multiple pieces of sashimi, and a roll of your choice. The Sunshine Roll, made with salmon, mango, and avocado, is fun for a sweet/savory combo, and the Austin FC Roll, made with a selection of green and black ingredients, is a nod to our professional soccer team.

Owners Také and Kayo have worked to create a restaurant that offers impeccable service and food, but at prices that are suitable for every day dining. (Meaning: This place won't break the bank.) The sake menu is robust, with a wide variety of sake available by the bottle or by the glass. If you're eating dinner with a crowd, order several plates of cold appetizers and fried or grilled dishes, lots of nigiri and sashimi, and a few rolls. Be sure to throw in a rice or noodle dish, like that yummy curry udon. Three or four plates per person is a good place to start. Almost everything on the menu is made to be shared, family-style.

> "Many items on our menu are straight from our own dining table at home, and our own family recipes. That way, customers get to have something we actually eat every day."
>
> —Kayo Asazu, owner of Komé

5 EAT DINNER AT AUSTIN'S OLDEST SEAFOOD COUNTER, QUALITY SEAFOOD MARKET

Right next to a busy highway, across the street from a dusty car lot, is **QUALITY SEAFOOD MARKET**, the oldest seafood market and restaurant in Austin, which has been impressing its guests since 1938. Judging by the crowds that consistently gather for midweek lunches, Friday happy hours, and weekend date-night dinners, the lack of elegance is happily overlooked. Maybe the no-frills interior even adds to the charm? I'm not sure, but what I do know is that they consistently deliver as one of the best casual seafood restaurants in Austin.

Quality Seafood is both a market and a restaurant. If you're looking to buy some fish to take home and cook, walk in the front door and head to the fish counter to your left, where a friendly fishmonger will tell you what's currently available. They only offer what is fresh and seasonal, so the options behind the glass are constantly changing. If you'd like to eat at the restaurant, walk up to the counter, place an order, and take a seat, and your food will be brought to you quickly. If you love oysters, you can sit at the oyster bar and watch them being shucked right in front of you. Take your pick of raw oysters from the Gulf or East Coast, or indulge in some grilled oysters Rockefeller, all warm and buttery. The po'boy sandwiches are a great bet for lunch: Your choice of filling is served on a toasty hoagie with lettuce and tomato. The seafood tacos with mango pineapple pico de gallo or the hearty bowl of seafood gumbo are other delicious lunch options. If you're stopping by for a celebratory dinner, Quality Seafood has all sorts of fresh seafood entrees like boiled snow crab clusters or grilled USA catfish with hush puppies and fried okra. Sip on some cold beer with your peel-and-eat shrimp, or order a simple house wine (remember, no frills here!) with a blackened Atlantic salmon.

6 ORDER A CRAFT COCKTAIL AT DRINKWELL

Cozy up to your date . . . this place is a treat! **DRINKWELL** is the neighborhood cocktail bar and gastropub that is unapologetically itself. The small room lends itself to an intimate date night or a dark and cozy place for a group of friends to meet up. Make a reservation for a table, especially if you're planning to stop by on a weekend evening. This isn't really the type of bar where you just waltz in and order. It's more of a sit-down experience, where you'll be escorted to a small table and given a handful of menus before a server takes your menu.

Yes, the cocktails are phenomenal. They're the primary reason this place won "Best New Bars in America" from *Food & Wine* magazine shortly after

they opened in 2012! But let's start with the food here, because that is, to me, the thing that makes this place incredibly special.

DrinkWell is often stuck under the misconception of being a cocktail bar, but it really is a neighborhood gastropub. The snacks and starters are perfect to pair with your drink, even if you don't plan on eating a full dinner here. Try the incredibly decadent hot whipped feta dip with bourbon-soaked dark cherry jam and a baguette, or a simple bowl of ancho-roasted chickpeas to munch while you sip your Old Fashioned. The DrinkWell burger is among the best in Austin, made with a blend of chuck and brisket and topped with house-made pickles on an Easy Tiger bun. And the dessert menu is tiny but hardly an afterthought. DrinkWell often takes nostalgic childhood favorites, like Cocoa Puffs, and turns them into a more sophisticated dessert item.

The cocktails are inventive and fun, yet completely approachable. You can start with the happy hour cocktail menu if you're looking for something simple. This is where DrinkWell offers discounts on seasonal classics like their Old Fashioned, gimlet, or dark & stormy. The menu rotates with the seasons, which means (a) you can always try something new, and (b) I'm not able to suggest anything in particular. But you don't need my help. The incredibly talented staff at DrinkWell will guide you in the right direction.

Of course, sometimes you just want a good old dive bar, and that's exactly where we're going next.

7 HANG OUT WITH THE LOCALS AT WORKHORSE BAR

Every neighborhood needs a standard dive bar where regulars can show up to see familiar faces while they enjoy a pint of beer or a well drink, and that's what **WORKHORSE BAR** is to the North Loop area. It's a dark, gritty bar with an Old West feel. Although it's open as early as 11 a.m., the tinted windows and dim lighting give it a snug and homey feel at all hours of the day or night. Walk in and find a seat at the bar, and you'll find a large tap wall that highlights local craft beer, as well as a selection of spirits for whatever stiff drink strikes your fancy. The bartenders and waitstaff are friendly, and the food is served quickly. Workhorse Bar's menu offers typical bar food, but it's prepared thoughtfully with high-quality ingredients. The burgers are big and dense and automatically cooked to medium; if you like a little pink in your burger, be sure to ask for medium rare. They're served with typical burger toppings and placed on grilled buns, which are a little toasty but still soft enough to soak up all the juicy and drippy goodness from the burger. If you're in Austin on a warm evening, there's no better place to enjoy a casual drink with friends (and your dog!) than Workhorse Bar's little back patio. This is the place for people who love hole-in-the-wall restaurants; no glitz, no glam, just a lot of regulars showing up to their local bar for a relaxing evening of burgers and beer.

THE BRENTWOOD CRAWL

1. Taste baked goods galore at **UPPER CRUST BAKERY**, 4508 BURNET RD., AUSTIN, (512) 467-0102, UPPERCRUSTBAKERY.COM

2. Kick off Saturday morning with a NY-style bagel sandwich at **NERVOUS CHARLIE'S**, 5501 N. LAMAR BLVD. STE. B101, AUSTIN, (512) 366-5305, NERVOUSCHARLIES.COM

3. Order biscuit sandwiches to-go at **BIRD BIRD BISCUIT**, 1401 W. KOENIG LN., AUSTIN, (512) 551-9820, BIRDBIRDBISCUIT.COM

4. Step inside the most darling French-inspired cafe and grocery, **ÉPICERIE**, 2307 HANCOCK DR., AUSTIN, (512) 371-6840, EPICERIEAUSTIN.COM

5. Indulge in pizza and award-winning beer at **PINTHOUSE PIZZA**, 4729 BURNET RD., AUSTIN, (512) 436-9605, PINTHOUSEPIZZA.COM

6. Enjoy an English afternoon tea at **BRENTWOOD SOCIAL HOUSE**, 1601 W. KOENIG LN., AUSTIN, (512) 362-8656, BRENTWOODSOCIAL.COM

7. Happy hour fusion fare at **THE PEACHED TORTILLA**, 5520 BURNET RD. STE. 100, AUSTIN, (512) 330-4439, THEPEACHEDTORTILLA.COM

8. Dine on interior Mexican cuisine at **FONDA SAN MIGUEL**, 2330 W. NORTH LOOP BLVD., AUSTIN, (512) 459-4121, FONDASANMIGUEL.COM

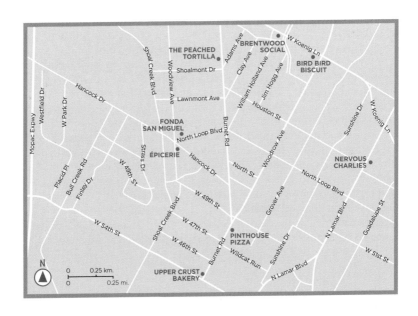

Brentwood

Family-Friendly Streets and Eats

AS WE MOVE FARTHER INTO NORTH AUSTIN, THE NEIGHBORHOOD lines get a bit blurrier. Allendale, Brentwood, and Crestview were farmlands when Austin was founded in the 1800s. As the city sprawled outward from downtown, these north Austin neighborhoods became prime real estate for buyers looking for single-family homes. And of course, as houses were built, restaurants popped up as well.

One of the major north/south streets in Austin is Burnet (pronounced "burn it"). This busy street has become a major food hub in north Austin. I considered calling this chapter the "Burnet Food Crawl," but there are just too many great restaurants up here! The crawl got too long and I had to split it into two separate neighborhoods: Brentwood and Crestview.

Brentwood has a fun mix of ranch-style homes and midcentury modern architecture. The sprawling lots make this a desirable place to buy a home because as Austin keeps growing, Brentwood seems to get closer to downtown Austin. And of course, the food scene in Allendale just keeps getting better and better.

1

TASTE BAKED GOODS GALORE AT UPPER CRUST BAKERY

Austin has a few local bakeries that everyone loves. If you're having a casual conversation and someone says, "hey, I need to order a cake for my mom's birthday, where should I go?", **UPPER CRUST BAKERY** is going to pop up in the running. (Other great options for ordering a whole cake: Quack's [see Hyde Park crawl], and Sugar Mama's [see Bouldin Creek crawl]). Upper Crust is a big, classic Austin bakery that has so much more going for it than just delicious pastries!

This is a rare find because the sprawling indoor space has two rooms for customers to sit and enjoy their pastries, and a large outdoor area with picnic tables for those gorgeous spring days in Austin. Book clubs gather for monthly get-togethers, friends meet up for afternoon coffee dates, and families bring in their little ones for a Saturday morning of good eats. This is a true neighborhood gem.

I must mention the cinnamon roll first, because it's not an intuitive item to order here. Most of us want gooey cinnamon rolls with a thick, melty layer of cream cheese frosting, but Upper Crust's cinnamon roll is unconventional and has no frosting. Don't think about it too hard; just order it and enjoy devouring the whole thing. The croissant-like dough is soft and fluffy with a swirl of chewy, caramelized cinnamon and sugar throughout. It's absolutely perfect with a hot black cup of coffee.

The cakes, pies, Danishes, croissants, and other pastries in the long pastry case are all worth tasting as well. I love ordering a tall slice of apple crumble pie on the first cold day of autumn. Thick chunks of apples are piled high inside a homemade pie dough and covered with a heavy sprinkling of cinnamon and sugar and roasted pecans. And if you have the occasion to order an entire cake, go to Upper Crust and order an irresistible mocha almond cake. Or if you don't have the occasion for it, just remember that "Tuesday" is a good enough reason.

Save some room for breakfast; our next stop is one of Austin's best bagel shops!

2 KICK OFF SATURDAY MORNING WITH A NY-STYLE BAGEL SANDWICH AT NERVOUS CHARLIE'S

Austin is a taco town. I've mentioned this approximately 35 times in this book, but we love tacos, we eat them daily, and we argue over who has the best tacos in Austin. But as this city grows and more and more folks move here from the Northeast, there has been an increasing demand for really, really good bagels. Enter: **NERVOUS CHARLIE'S.**

Co-owners Chris and Ali realized there weren't many places in Austin to get authentic, NY-style bagels. We're talking about the type that are dense on the outside, warm and fluffy on the inside, and the perfect vehicle for house-made cream cheese or big, hearty breakfast sandwiches. So they opened Nervous Charlie's Bagel Shop, named after their happy-yet-nervous-at-all-times Cavalier King Charles spaniel.

These bagels are knock-your-socks-off delicious. Take your pick of bagel flavor (a classic everything bagel is a great place to start) and then choose a cream cheese flavor (they have so many flavors, like plain, scallion, strawberry, honey walnut, pistachio, and a spicy arbol and *pequin* pepper).

But if you know your way around an authentic bagel shop menu and you're ready to dive into a heartier breakfast, try one of their classic breakfast sandwiches. No need to get too fancy here: just pick your bagel flavor,

choose a protein (I love Taylor Ham for that yummy saltiness), and they'll pile on two fried eggs and melted cheese.

You can order at the counter or place your order online so it's ready when you arrive. Their cafe has a few little tables where guests can enjoy their bagels, or you can ask to get it wrapped up and all ready to-go.

My go-to order? A toasted salt bagel with bacon, fried eggs, and cheese. I don't know if it was a salt deficiency during pregnancy (I mean . . . sure . . . let's just call it that), but I craved this thing all the time during my third trimester with my second child. And you'd better believe I indulged!

Next up is one more breakfast stop. I just can't help myself . . . there are so many good breakfast stops in Brentwood!

3 ORDER BISCUIT SANDWICHES TO-GO AT BIRD BIRD BISCUIT

When the craving for absolutely decadent biscuit breakfast sandwiches hits ya, there's no better place to go than **BIRD BIRD BISCUIT**. Sure, it's a cute name, but these are serious sandwiches. (As in, show up very hungry!) This Brentwood location of Bird Bird Biscuit has a walk-up window. You can order your food and then waltz up to the window to quickly grab it, making this stop a great one when you're in a hurry.

Friends and co-owners Brian and Ryan worked on hundreds of batches of biscuits to get them just right, and the result is pretty impressive. They're sturdy enough to hold up the hefty breakfast toppings, yet still soft and fluffy.

The Queen Beak is definitely the way to go if it's your first time here. This breakfast (or anytime!) sandwich includes a spiced and breaded chicken breast that's drizzled with cayenne black pepper honey. It's served on one of those famous warm biscuits, which has been slathered with bacon-infused chipotle mayo. It's a little bit sweet, a little bit spicy, and a whole lotta delicious.

If you're not into fried chicken sandwiches, they also have other options, like a simple free-range egg over medium with a slice of melty cheddar cheese, or the popular Bird Bird Bacon, one of their breakfast bestsellers.

Top your biscuit with bacon or veggie sausage or just eat it plain with butter and jam, but be sure to grab a few extra biscuits to bring home for breakfast the next day, too. Once you have your first bite of a Bird Bird Biscuit, you're never going back!

4

STEP INSIDE THE MOST DARLING FRENCH-INSPIRED CAFE AND GROCERY, ÉPICERIE

Ok, I lied. I'm listing yet one more breakfast option! **ÉPICERIE** is a really popular brunch spot in Austin because it checks off all of the boxes: delectable French/Louisiana-inspired cuisine, a beautiful, bright dining space, a charming outdoor patio, and a sweet little grocery store where you can shop for wine, chocolate, candles, and other delicacies. It feels a little bit like you're dining inside a neighborhood grocery store . . . which makes sense, since épicerie means "grocery store" in French. This is where the Austin brunch crowd loves to linger.

Chef Sarah McIntosh serves her food in a setting that inspires rest and relaxation. Épicerie doesn't accept reservations, so pop in, order a cup of

coffee, and enjoy a lazy start to your morning; there's a good chance you'll have to wait around before you can snag a table during peak brunch hours. (It will be worth the wait, though.) Be sure to start with something from the pastry case, like a *pain au chocolat* or a *kouign amann.* (Oh, and while you're at it, order one of those salted chocolate chip cookies to bring home and enjoy after your meal—they're the best in Austin!)

The quiche of the day + salad is an excellent place to start. Since the bakery program is what makes this place really shine, the quiche crust is perfect, with a flaky, buttery crust. And speaking of butter, I adore their croissants, whether I'm eating them plain or I order the breakfast croissant sandwich with sausage, egg, aioli, jalapeño, and cheddar. It's a simple breakfast

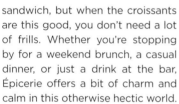

sandwich, but when the croissants are this good, you don't need a lot of frills. Whether you're stopping by for a weekend brunch, a casual dinner, or just a drink at the bar, Épicerie offers a bit of charm and calm in this otherwise hectic world.

And I'm going to say it again, just to make sure you heard me: If you're visiting Austin, the cookies make great plane snacks to enjoy on your trip back home!

5

INDULGE IN PIZZA AND AWARD-WINNING BEER AT PINTHOUSE PIZZA

There's no shortage of excellent pizza in Austin, and we also have our fair share of award-winning breweries. PINTHOUSE PIZZA combines the two. This is the place to go if you love fresh, hazy IPAs and big, chewy-crust pizzas. This is also a great place to go if you're all about eating with a crowd. The interior is full of long rows of tables and benches, so you can order a bunch of pies, a few pints of beer, and enjoy a big meal with all of your friends.

Pinthouse's beer is a hop-lover's dream. They've long been obsessed with big, bold, hoppy profiles, but they work hard to balance them to create drinkable beers that keep customers coming back again and again. They've won medals at the fiercest beer competitions in the country for their IPAs. If you're into hoppy beers, you've probably already heard of Electric Jellyfish. It's Pinthouse's flagship New England IPA, and it's packed with citrus notes and lots of haze. This is the beer you're most likely to find on any random draft list on Austin. Whether you're cheering on Austin FC at Q2 Stadium, enjoying a ribeye at a local steakhouse, or stopping at an airport bar for a quick drink before your flight—Electric Jellyfish will be there. Looking for a dark beer? Try the Bearded Seal dry Irish stout, a bold and roasty beer with notes of coffee and dark

chocolate. This beer won a gold medal at the Great American Beer Festival. And don't discount their pilsners, or their other IPAs, barrel-aged stouts, and porters. Pinthouse is a beer powerhouse and they've won awards in nearly every category.

When you're ready to order a pizza, pay at the counter, take a seat, and your pizza will be delivered hot and fresh to your table. The Ooh La La is a pepperoni and cheese pie covered with a pile of fresh baby arugula, peppadew peppers, and a drizzle of spicy local honey. It's the perfect combination of spicy and sweet. And if you're a traditionalist in your pizza approach, you can't go wrong with the pepperoni and basil pizza. I've paired that with a Green Battles IPA more times than I can count, and I don't plan on stopping any time soon.

6

ENJOY AN ENGLISH AFTERNOON TEA AT BRENTWOOD SOCIAL HOUSE

This adorable bungalow-turned-coffee house in the heart of Brentwood is one of the only places in Austin where you can find such a vast selection of English pastries. If you're searching for Bakewell tarts, scones, and Millionaire's Bars, this is the place to get them. Owner Sarah is originally from England, and she's the baking mastermind behind all the gorgeous pastries in the pastry case.

Before it was a cafe, the building that now holds **BRENTWOOD SOCIAL HOUSE** was a clothing boutique. And before that? Well, walk through the front door and you'll be able to see the bones of the original house. This means that there are multiple rooms where you can snuggle in with a scone and a cup of tea and get some work done, crack open a good book, or connect with a friend.

Beyond the vast selection of coffee, loose leaf tea, and wine, Brentwood Social House offers a traditional English

afternoon tea (or "high tea"), complete with a three-tiered stand of sweet and savory pastries, a lace tablecloth and flower, and vintage tableware. This is available for either adults or children, and it's a popular birthday party idea in north Austin.

Speaking of children, this darling cafe is a wonderful spot to stop by if you're in Austin with young children. There's a room in the back that's dedicated to children's books and a toy kitchen, so you can order a cuppa and relax while your little one plays nearby. There's also a playscape in the backyard that's very popular among school-aged children in the afternoons.

7 HAPPY HOUR FUSION FARE AT THE PEACHED TORTILLA

Do you remember back in the Zilker chapter when I was saying that there's a pattern of awesome Austin food trucks turning into brick and mortars? **THE PEACHED TORTILLA** is another great example of that. I'm telling you—we Austinites have mad respect for chefs who dream up a creative menu, invest in a rinky-dink little truck, and work their tails off for a few hot Texas summers and then grow enough of a crowd to expand from there. If you do all of that work, we'll support you when you open your storefront.

The Peached Tortilla serves Southern food fused with the Asian flavors that chef Eric Silverstein

grew up on. This is, quite simply, fusion food that will make almost anyone feel really happy. At its core, The Peached Tortilla pays homage to Asian street food. The menu is approachable but has a grown-up twist. For instance: Instead of serving a basic chicken wing, they make theirs with a fish sauce vinaigrette, herbs, and shallots. The Japajam Burger is a 6-ounce patty with all the stops: pepperjack cheese, fried egg, tempura onion strings, and Chinese barbecue sauce. (Psst: Be sure to snap a picture of this one to post on the 'gram before you dive in! It's a beautiful burger.) Their rendition of the traditional Cantonese dish beef chow fun, the Southern Fun, is a big bowl full of delicious flavors: braised brisket, kale, bean sprouts, and wide rice noodles.

> "The Austin food scene has changed dramatically in the past decade. It is night-and-day different. I remember if you wanted to eat Thai food or Italian food, you only had one or two options in town. Now you have eight to ten. It's a whole new ball game. Money is flowing in from every direction that is being used to open restaurants. If you spend a million dollars on a build out, you're no longer the exception to the rule, you are the rule. You have to adapt and keep pushing, or ultimately, you will be forgotten."
>
> —Chef/owner Eric Silverstein, The Peached Tortilla

Basically a party in your mouth. The Peached Tortilla is a small restaurant, but it's bright and beautiful and a lovely place to meet up with coworkers for happy hour. Whether you're stopping by for brunch, cocktails, or a full-blown meal, be sure to try the instantly addicting charred brussels with bacon jam and Parmesan. You'll thank me later.

8 DINE ON INTERIOR MEXICAN CUISINE AT FONDA SAN MIGUEL

FONDA SAN MIGUEL is recognized as one of the best interior Mexican cuisine restaurants in the country. It's been around since 1975, so rather than being hot and trendy, this place is timeless. The walls are covered in museum-quality artwork, and bright tiles and showstopping plants flow from room to room. This restaurant truly is one of the most stunning places to eat in Austin. Tom Gilliland and the late Miguel Ravago introduced authentic regional Mexican cuisine to Austin back when there were very few interior Mexican restaurants in the United States and Mexican food meant gluey enchiladas topped with yellow cheese. Fonda San Miguel has changed our approach to Mexican food. My best tip for dining here: Arrive as hungry as you can, because you'll want to taste everything.

The cocktail menu features bright and beautiful classics. Fonda San Miguel is known for their tequila and mezcal-based drinks, but they also offer gin-based coolers, a frozen and creamy "Fonda colada," and their own take on a sophisticated espresso martini.

The dinner menu has so many beautiful dishes, I hardly know where to start for suggestions. (Try them all!) If I must pick a few favorites, the tacos al pastor are a great place to start. One serving will give you four tacos that are full of melt-in-your-mouth pork meat and two homemade sauces. The fresh ceviches are all wonderful, as is the *queso fundido,* made with house-made pork chorizo, swiss chard, and served with homemade tortillas. The *cochinita pibil,* a Yucatan specialty of pork baked in a banana leaf, is so exceptionally soft and flavorful, you probably won't be able to stop eating. But try to save a bit of space for *camarones en crema de chipotle*

(that's "shrimp in spicy chipotle cream sauce," for anyone who's rusty on their high school Spanish language skills), or their *pollo en mole poblano,* a baked one-quarter chicken in the traditional mole of Puebla. As I said before: There are so many fantastic things to taste here, you'll want to arrive as hungry as possible. Please don't leave without trying the *tres leches* cake. Enjoy every delectable morsel!

THE CRESTVIEW CRAWL

1. Dine at the ultimate neighborhood pizza and sandwich shop, **LITTLE DELI & PIZZERIA**, 7101 WOODROW AVE. STE. A, AUSTIN, (512) 467-7302, LITTLEDELIANDPIZZA.COM

2. Take on the heat with Nashville-style chicken at **T22 CHICKEN JOINT**, 7211 BURNET RD., AUSTIN, (512) 520-1998, TUMBLE22.COM

3. Bring your pup to **YARD BAR**, 6700 BURNET RD., AUSTIN, (512) 900-3773, YARDBAR.COM

4. Celebrate nostalgia at **TOP NOTCH HAMBURGERS**, 7525 BURNET RD., AUSTIN, (512) 452-2181, TOPNOTCHAUSTIN.COM

5. Take time for an ice cream break at **LICK**, 7525 BURNET RD., AUSTIN, (512) 452-2181, TOPNOTCHAUSTIN.COM

6. Finish your evening with a bottle of wine and tinned sardines at **VIOLET CROWN WINE BAR AND COFFEE SHOP**, 7100 WOODROW AVE. STE. 100, AUSTIN, (512) 215-0085, THEVIOLETCROWNATX.COM

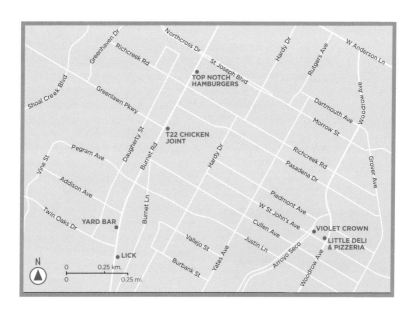

Crestview

Crawling through North Austin

IF YOU FIND YOURSELF IN FAR NORTH AUSTIN FOR THE DAY, Crestview is a cute neighborhood where you can enjoy an afternoon of strolling and eating. It was developed in the 1950s and 60s on dairy farm land, and now it's full of bungalows with big backyards, modern rebuilds, and quiet(ish) streets . . . at least for now. I mean, haven't we established that Austin is growing and sprawling at a rapid pace? Even though Crestview used to be considered living in "way far north Austin," it's now a very desirable location. At just about 8 miles north of downtown, you can reach the city in about 20 minutes. But beyond the proximity to skyscrapers, Crestview is one of my favorite places in north Austin because of the adorable eateries I'm going to share with you.

I'm going to try not to call every restaurant a "neighborhood gem" even though I really want to. So many of these fantastic coffee shops, dinner spots, and bars are tucked right into neighborhoods, making them highly walkable destinations that local Crestview residents frequent.

Another great part about north Austin is that, as Austin keeps growing, more and more restaurants are choosing to open their second or third locations up north. So if you live in Crestview or you're visiting and staying in a vacation rental here, there's a good chance you'll be able to hit up some of the Austin restaurants you might have missed earlier in this book.

1

DINE AT THE ULTIMATE NEIGHBORHOOD PIZZA AND SANDWICH SHOP, LITTLE DELI & PIZZERIA

LITTLE DELI & PIZZERIA is a cherished neighborhood spot for its hand-tossed New Jersey pies and massive menu of hot and cold subs. It's a very walkable destination for Crestview neighborhood residents as it's nestled right at the end of the Crestview shopping center. The lunch game is strong here, folks. Order your pizza at the counter, and the friendly staff will bring it to your table (if you're lucky enough to snag one . . . this place gets crowded at lunch!). The thin, hand-tossed pizza is cooked on a 2-inch stone hearth, served brown and crisp yet still soft enough to fold in half. You can order a single slice for just a couple bucks if you're dining solo, or an entire pie if you're with a group. The sandwiches are made with the highest quality bread, meats, and cheeses, which are obviously a must-have for any great sandwich. This is a no-frills deli with all of the classic sandwiches you'd expect to find: BLT, turkey and swiss, meatball sub, and classic pastrami, among many others. One of their more unusual menu items is Harry's Perfect Pastrami, a big, drippy, delicious mess of half a pound of hot top-round pastrami, Thousand Island dressing, and fresh coleslaw. It's griddled and served warm and toasty on rye bread.

Be sure to get one of the chewy chocolate cookies on your way out the door! They're baked in-house every day and taste like a mix of a rich, chewy brownie and a crisp chocolate cookie, with big chunks of walnuts interspersed in the caramelized chocolate cookie.

Hungry for more? Hot fried chicken is next!

2 TAKE ON THE HEAT WITH NASHVILLE-STYLE CHICKEN AT T22 CHICKEN JOINT

Heat lovers, get ready: **T22** fried chicken is a seriously spicy indulgence! What started as a popular food truck in Austin has grown to open multiple restaurant locations, and the brick and mortar in north Austin is the perfect lunch stop on your Crestview food crawl. T22's fried chicken is coated in chef Harold Marmulstein's own secret blend of spices and is available in six heat levels. Start by choosing your chicken (white/dark/mixed, chicken sandwiches, or tenders), and then pick a heat level:

1. Painless
2. Hot
3. Mo' hot
4. Dang hot
5. Cluckin' hot
6. Stupid hot

Once you take that first bite, there's no going back. This is for two reasons: (1) T22 fried chicken is ridiculously addicting, and (2) if you choose the hottest level, you might pay tomorrow. . . . Regardless of the spice level you choose, you're in for a treat with this crispy coating and juicy meat. The O.G. Classic Chicken Sandwich is just that: a classic chicken sandwich without too many frills. If it ain't broke, you know? It's a simple fried chicken breast topped with kale slaw, bread and butter pickles, and Duke's mayo. Make it a Southern Chicken Sandwich by swapping the chicken breast for a thigh. The salads, sides, and desserts are all

heavenly. The Hot Chicken Cobb Salad is just right when you want some greens but you also want to eat something a little bit more fun. The potato salad, barbecue beans, and mac-and-cheese are the perfect accompaniments to make it into a Southern feast. Don't miss out on the pies, too. Between the Mile-High Lemon Meringue and Pecan Chocolate Toffee, you're sure to find the perfect sweet treat to wrap up your meal.

3 BRING YOUR PUP TO YARD BAR

If you find yourself in Austin with a pup who has some energy to burn, head over to **YARD BAR**, where you can set your canine loose to play and frolic in the off-leash dog park while you enjoy a drink with friends! A small cover charge will let your furry friend into the safely guarded, fenced-in dog park where dozens of happy animals are chasing each other around. And while the dogs are having fun socializing, owners can bond over a drink and a bite of food.

There are plenty of picnic tables and lawn chairs for the humans to sit and observe all the craziness. A bar with a nice selection of local and national craft beer and a variety of cocktails should fulfill all your imbibing needs. While the dog park and bar are for 21+ only, all ages are welcome at the adjacent dining patio, where you can order burgers, salads, sandwiches, and even house-made dog treats.

4 CELEBRATE NOSTALGIA AT TOP NOTCH HAMBURGERS

Alright, alright, alright . . . **TOP NOTCH HAMBURGERS** has been slinging patties since 1971 and made its claim to fame by being featured in the 1993 film *Dazed and Confused.* This is one of the few vintage drive-ins that still offers curbside service, although there's also a full dining room for guests who want to dine in. The lunch crowd is a steady stream of regulars who have been eating here for decades, as well as tourists who want to see the famous restaurant where the characters in *Dazed and Confused* stopped for food before their big night out. Top Notch's menu is pretty basic: They offer burgers, fried chicken, and a few other sandwich options. The bestseller is the basic cheeseburger: a charcoal-grilled patty with mayo, cheese, tomato, lettuce, pickles, and onions. If you're looking for something uniquely Austin, try the Longhorn Special, which comes with double meat and special sauce. The

fried chicken menu is kept simple: You'll choose dark, white, or mixed meat, and add on a couple sides. Take your pick of sides from all the drive-in classics: fried onion rings, mashed potatoes and gravy, sweet buttered corn, tots, fries, or okra. There aren't a lot of frills at this restaurant, but since they've been in business since 1971, they obviously don't need them.

One of my favorite parts about this hot rod hangout is ordering a chocolate malt at the end of the meal. There aren't many places that offer thick and creamy chocolate malts, and I adore them. I have so many fond memories of going to old-school diners with my dad when I was a child and ordering a kid-size malt and curly fries. It brings back lots of memories to slurp on a delicious malt at Top Notch, except now that I'm the adult and paying for it, I order whatever size I want!

You don't have to Instagram your food here and tag #AustinFoodCrawls, but . . . it'd be a lot cooler if you did.

5

TAKE TIME FOR AN ICE CREAM BREAK AT LICK

I've mentioned this before, but it bears repeating: Texas and ice cream go hand in hand. I grew up eating Blue Bell, a popular Texas grocery store brand, and my family would have no fewer than five tubs of it in our outdoor freezer on any given day. I remember walking downstairs late at night as a child to get a glass of water and seeing my dad sitting at the kitchen table, eating directly out of the half-gallon container of Moolinium Crunch to get every last little bit.

Austin has our own ice cream brands, and one of the biggest and most popular among them is **LICK HONEST ICE CREAMS**. Keeping true to the Austin culture, Lick cares about sourcing milk and cream from Mill-King Creamery near Waco, Texas, providing seasonal flavors and offering vegan options in their artisanal ice cream. Their Hill Country Honey and Vanilla Bean is made with local Good Flow honey, and the Mexican Plum Jam & Chocolate has thick crumbles of dark chocolate from SRSLY chocolate. I could go on and on about the ridiculously tasty flavors, but you just have to get there and try them for yourself; the proof is in the taste! The delectable flavors are true and strong. Lick only uses ingredients that are in season in Texas, so the sweet peaches you're tasting in the summer won't be available in December, when peaches don't naturally grow in Austin. Another

THE BEST-SELLING EVERYDAY FLAVORS AT LICK HONEST ICE CREAMS

Caramel Salt Lick

Texas Sheet Cake

Goat Cheese Thyme & Honey

Roasted Beets & Fresh Mint

fun thing about Lick: Regular flavors are packaged and sold in certain grocery stores, so you can try them even if you're not able to make it to a scoop shop. When I'm grocery shopping, I'll often throw a pint of Lick's Texas Sheet Cake ice cream in my grocery cart so that I can enjoy it at home, too.

6

FINISH YOUR EVENING WITH A BOTTLE OF WINE AND TINNED SARDINES AT VIOLET CROWN WINE BAR AND COFFEE SHOP

Well, for all the hoopla I make about Crestview being considered "close to downtown" now by Austin residents who live north of Palmer Lane, **VIOLET CROWN WINE BAR AND COFFEE SHOP** is giving the Brentwood neighborhood residents a reason to, well, never venture to downtown Austin. Because why drive south when you can walk to get a perfect morning *cortado* and a locally made doughnut? Or enjoy a tinned fish and caviar and potato chips with a crisp glass of Gruner Veltliner, produced naturally and poured by a kindhearted bartender with a smile?

Husbands Chris and Grant opened Violet Crown to be a spot to serve the local community. They serve only natural wines here—and no, that doesn't necessarily mean they only have "funky" wines at Violet Crown. It just means their wine menu features wine that was made without manipulative farming like the addition of herbicides and pesticides. Natural wine is a little bit better for you and a little bit better for our planet.

My favorite part about Violet Crown is that it's an all-day affair. The light-filled shop is just as wonderful in the morning when you want a macchiato and a chocolate croissant as it is in the evening when you want to meet with a friend and share a bottle of New Zealand pinot noir. The drink menu features an exciting selection of wine by-the-glass, and you can also venture to their bottle shop and enjoy any purchased bottles onsite for a small bottle charge.

In addition to being a thriving coffee and wine bar with morning and evening snacky menus available, Violet Crown also features a wine club. This is part of the "community-building" component that the owners wanted to highlight. Members get to try new and exciting wines, and they also get to partake in a monthly pick-up party at Violet Crown.

Whether you're stopping by in the morning for a latte and a solo journaling session, or you want to meet up for an evening date and enjoy a bottle of bubbles paired with a cheese board, Violet Crown is the neighborhood spot that just seems to hit just right at any time of the day.

THE GEORGETOWN CRAWL

1. Start your morning at **SWEET LEMON KITCHEN**, 812 S. CHURCH ST., GEORGETOWN, (512) 270-0812, SWEETLEMONKITCHEN.COM

2. Order Georgetown's best pizza at **600 DEGREES PIZZERIA**, 124 E. 8TH ST., GEORGETOWN, (512) 943-9272, 600DEGREESPIZZERIA.COM

3. Get some birra at **MIKEY V'S ON THE SQUARE**, 112 W. 8TH ST., GEORGETOWN, (512) 688-1249, MIKEYVSTACOS.COM

4. Time for a caffeine pick-me-up at **309 COFFEE**, 309 S. MAIN ST., GEORGETOWN, (512) 931-4990, 309.COFFEE

5. Roadside eats at Georgetown's iconic **MONUMENT CAFE**, 500 S. AUSTIN AVE., GEORGETOWN, (512) 930-9586, THEMONUMENTCAFE.COM

6. Enjoy margaritas and queso at **EL MONUMENTO**, 205 W. 2ND ST., GEORGETOWN, (512) 591-7866, ELMONUMENTOGEORGETOWN.COM

7. Finish the night with cocktails at **THE GOLDEN RULE**, 606 S. CHURCH ST., GEORGETOWN, (512) 843-5900, GOLDENRULEGTX.COM

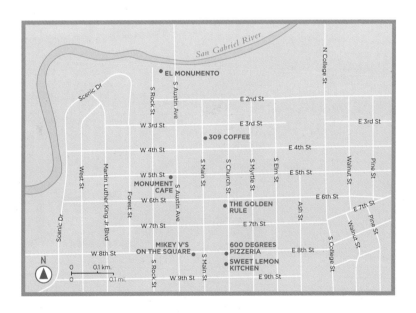

Georgetown

The Most Beautiful Town Square in Texas

HISTORIC GEORGETOWN, TEXAS, HAS EARNED A SPOT IN AUSTIN
Food Crawls, despite being 25 miles north and in an entirely different
county than the city of Austin. Why are we talking about Georgetown?
Well, because it's a beautiful little day trip from Austin, and it has become
quite a foodie destination! Plus, if you're visiting Austin and driving down
from north Texas, you'll go right through Georgetown. Use this chapter
to find a fun place to stop on the way. And if you live in Georgetown . . .
lucky you! I hope this inspires you to get out and explore the amazing local
restaurants in your own charming town square.

Georgetown is known as the Red Poppy Capital of Texas. It's one of the
few locations in the United States where poppies reseed themselves from
year to year, and they grow naturally during the months of March and April.
There's even a Poppy Festival in Georgetown every spring.

My friends who live in Georgetown tell me that they rarely have to venture out of Georgetown and make the 25-mile drive to Austin to visit great
restaurants, because they have so many amazing options within their own
sweet town.

Get ready for a fun day of eating your way through Georgetown, Texas.

1

START YOUR MORNING AT SWEET LEMON KITCHEN

SWEET LEMON KITCHEN will most likely be bustling with smiling staff members taking orders, local Georgetown residents greeting friends and giving hugs, and servers running plates to tables. It's that type of adorable cafe where you can meet your sister for a morning coffee date, bring a laptop for a solo morning of work, or gather with a group of friends for a casual weekday lunch. It's a fresh, casual, and oh-so-charming cafe created by local Georgetown resident Rachel Cummins. The farm-to-table goodies are familiar, but elevated. Try a delicious croissant sandwich for breakfast, served on their freshly baked sliced croissants with melty cheddar cheese, egg and crisp bacon, roasted tomato, and a tasty garlic aioli. If you're stopping by for breakfast, their cinnamon roll might be the most popular item on the menu! It's perfectly soft and pillowy and smothered in decadent cream cheese frosting. These always sell out, so get there early if you have your heart set on one. (I was too late to get one the first time I visited, and it ruined the rest of my day. Just kidding . . . kind of.)

Lunch includes panini sandwiches that are served with fruit and chips, salads, and soups (try the Sweet Lemon house salad but add a scoop of their chicken salad!), and even smaller plates for little ones who might be visiting with you. Sweet Lemon Kitchen's pastries are my favorite things on the menu, so I won't judge you if you stop by quickly for a coffee and a seasonal scone with butter and jam, or a slice of their cinnamon swirl coffee cake with pecan streusel. After all, there are so many places we need to visit in Georgetown!

2 ORDER GEORGETOWN'S BEST PIZZA AT 600 DEGREES PIZZERIA

Ask anyone for the best pizza in Georgetown, and they'll send you to **600 DEGREES PIZZERIA**. It's just off the Georgetown square, and it's typically packed with visitors and locals alike. They've been open since 2014, serving craft beer, wings, and North Beach pizza in their vintage building.

Definitely order some of their famous wings—they're the best in Georgetown! They come in a bunch of flavors, but the taco and the teriyaki are my personal favorites. Of course, there are classic

flavors like ranch and lemon pepper, but I say just live a little and try something new! The gourmet cheese bread is insane—it's hot fluffy crust topped with a cheesy topping, so you can just think of it as a pizza warmup.

And then the pizza is the main event. If you decide to order it by the slice, be prepared . . . the slices are enormous! One slice will typically fill me up.

Keep in mind 600 Degrees is a really small restaurant, so it can get pretty crowded on the weekends. If you don't want to have to wait for a table, order your pizza ahead for carry-out. These pies are delicious no matter where you eat them.

3 GET SOME BIRRIA AT MIKEY V'S ON THE SQUARE

Do you ever find yourself craving birria? I do. Like, on a regular basis! But there aren't a lot of taco shops that offer it. Thankfully, **MIKEY V'S ON THE SQUARE** has some of the best dang birria tacos, beef birria quesadillas, and even birria ramen in the entire greater Austin area!

This little taco shop is on the historic town square, but to find it you first have to walk through a hot sauce shop. (Go ahead and buy a bottle while you're walking through—these hot sauces are so good!) Once you get to the taco shop you can place an order at the counter and find a seat. Your food will be brought to you pretty quickly, all hot and fresh.

The beef birria taco features slow-cooked beef in a grilled corn tortilla. It's served with a cup of consommé, the spicy, velvety sauce that's left behind after the meat has cooked. You can dip your taco in this, or just use a spoon and sip it like soup.

And what is birria ramen, you ask? Well, think of a regular cup of ramen noodles (yeah, the cheap stuff that got you through college), but add 6 ounces of that hearty beef birria and swap out consommé instead of water. Truly delicious.

4

TIME FOR A CAFFEINE PICK-ME-UP AT 309 COFFEE

Lots of small towns aren't lucky enough to have a coffee shop this great, but Georgetown has been blessed with **309 COFFEE**, named after their address on South Main Street. This shop is cozy and welcoming and the perfect place to rest or work, but they don't rely on their charming environment alone. 309 Coffee is serious about their coffee craft, sourcing beans from some of the country's most reputable coffee roasters, as well as roasting their own house blend at their nearby roastery. Order a custom-made pour-over or a beautiful cappuccino and pair it with a salted dark chocolate cookie or your favorite breakfast pastry.

309 Coffee stays open into the evening when you can order a glass of wine or a pint of beer. With both indoor and outdoor seating, this little shop is the perfect place to slow down and enjoy a conversation before we head off to our next stop.

5

ROADSIDE EATS AT GEORGETOWN'S ICONIC MONUMENT CAFE

MONUMENT CAFE is a 1940s-style classic diner in the heart of Georgetown. It's been featured in plenty of national publications, including *Diners, Drive-ins and Dives,* but the fame hasn't gone to its head; Monument Cafe is still family-owned and makes everything from scratch.

The menu has a lot of classic diner fare, but with a few Tex-Mex twists thrown in for good measure. If it's your first time visiting AND you're really hungry, start with the chicken and biscuits. The two buttermilk biscuits are grilled and served open-face, so they have a bit of a char on them. Then they're topped with a crispy fried chicken breast, two eggs, and a big heap of Monument Cafe's homemade sausage gravy.

And pretty much anyone will tell you to be sure and try the chicken fried steak for lunch! Yes, it really is that good. But I also love some of their healthier options, like their tasty salads, the soup of the day (last time I was there it was a tomato bisque), and hearty turkey and, my favorite, the turkey, bacon, and avocado sandwich. I like to get mine with sweet potato fries on the side.

This place is sooo good, they decided to open a sister restaurant! That's where we're heading next.

6

ENJOY MARGARITAS AND QUESO AT EL MONUMENTO

Even though it's from the same owners as Monument Cafe, **EL MONUMENTO** is an entirely different experience. It's a contemporary 7,700-square-foot Mexican restaurant with four separate dining areas and an interior courtyard. The landscaping features dry-weather plants that are indigenous to south Texas, adding to the Tex-Mex flair.

Happy hour is a great time to stop by El Monumento for a cocktail and some *queso flameado*. It's basically a big skillet filled with melty cheese and *rajas*, served with housemade corn tortillas. I love to pair this with their jalapeño margarita—it comes with a nice amount of spicy *tajin* on the rim.

El Monumento leans a bit more "Mex" than "Tex," meaning you'll find plenty of authentic Mexican dishes here and not as much ground beef and cheddar cheese (as you'd expect at a Tex-Mex). Dive into the plates of small Mexican street tacos, delicious tortas Cubanos, and chile rellenos.

El Monumento is a very popular restaurant. But thankfully, it's a huge space and can accommodate a crowd!

7

FINISH THE NIGHT WITH COCKTAILS AT THE GOLDEN RULE

There's no better place to finish our Georgetown food crawl than **THE GOLDEN RULE**, an energetic cocktail bar and restaurant just off the downtown square. The motto here is "above all else: goodwill, friendship, and kind regard," and that's exactly how you'll be treated when you walk in the door. Cozy up at the bar and you'll soon be greeted by a kind bartender with a smile who's ready to prepare a cocktail for you. Worth noting: If you choose to stop by earlier in the day, The Golden Rule has excellent discounts during happy hour.

Try the refreshing Death by 1,000 Berries, made with tequila, lemon juice, simple syrup, strawberry, mint, and Liquid Death sparkling water. It's perfectly refreshing on a hot Texas day. Or work your way through any of

the other excellent craft cocktails on the menu. They also offer plenty of craft beer and wine by the glass and bottle.

The Golden Rule is much more than a cocktail bar! The American food menu features delicious apps (try those carne asada fries if you're feeling munchy!), salads, burgers, grilled entrees, and yummy desserts.

Whether you're heading out for a night on the town or you just want a comfortable place to enjoy a burger and an Old Fashioned, The Golden Rule is always going to treat you well.

THE BUDA CRAWL

1. Coffee, tacos, and good vibes at **PROGRESS COFFEE + BEER**, 750 FM2001, BUDA, (512) 434-3904, PROGRESSCOFFEE.COM/HOME/BUDA

2. It's all about Cajun food at **MUDBUGS**, 306 S. MAIN ST. STE. 107, BUDA, (512) 523-8241, PEACELOVEANDCRAWFISH.COM

3. Steak and seafood at **TASTE ON MAIN**, 116 MAIN ST., BUDA, (512) 957-8991, TASTEONMAIN.COM

4. Nightcaps and fireside chats at **NATE'S COFFEE & COCKTAILS**, 306 S. MAIN ST. STE. 101, BUDA, (512) 523-8256, NATES-BUDA.COM

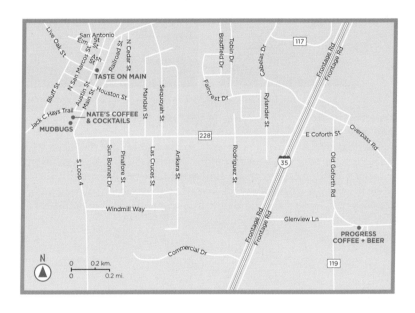

Buda

It's Called "Byoo-da"

WE'RE LEAVING TRAVIS COUNTY AND AUSTIN ONCE AGAIN, but this time we're going south to Buda, Texas. This historic town (hey, 1881 is considered historic for Texas) is oh-so-charming and makes an excellent little day trip from Austin. With annual events like their December Trail of Lights and a 4th of July fireworks extravaganza, there's a lot of character and community in this small town.

If you're visiting for the day, you'll want to spend most of your time in the nationally recognized historic downtown area. It's only 6 city blocks, but it's packed with boutique shops, art stores, local spas, and plenty of fun places to eat. (We'll circle back to the food in a moment!)

Buda is growing FAST! At just about 15 miles south of downtown, lots of folks are moving here for its family-friendly community and proximity to downtown. And it's so much more than a commuter city these days. Back in the day, a lot of homebuyers would choose to live in Buda so they could have a larger, newer house at a fraction of Austin's prices, and then commute into downtown Austin for work. But ever since the COVID-19 pandemic caused remote work to become the new normal, parents and employees are finding there's no longer reason to leave Buda every morning at 7 a.m.

And with this many great places to eat? Well, now there's really no reason to leave Buda! This town boasts an incredible Cajun eatery, a couple cute coffee shops, and several other destination-worthy restaurants that are great for lunch or dinner. I'm so excited to show you the best eats in Buda!

1

COFFEE, TACOS, AND GOOD VIBES AT PROGRESS COFFEE + BEER

There's definitely a need for a family-friendly hangout spot in a city like Buda, and thankfully **PROGRESS COFFEE + BEER** delivers. This all-day coffee shop, beer garden, and cocktail bar provides a comfy spot to gather with friends and family.

Stop by in the morning for a cappuccino and a croissant. They get all their pastries from Easy Tiger, one of Austin's tried and true bakeries. Feeling hungry? Head outside and order a few breakfast tacos from a food truck.

As the day rolls on, Progress Coffee caters to families with little ones who need space to run around. There are ample picnic tables outside

where parents can sit and enjoy a local draft beer while the kids play on the adjacent playscape. Maybe you're visiting solo and just looking for a quiet place to get some reading done? Enjoy the fresh air on their outdoor deck, which is on the opposite side of the building from all the playground noise.

In the evening hours you might walk in to hear live music being performed on the small corner stage. You can grab a spot at the bar, order a craft cocktail, and enjoy some food from one of the food trucks outside.

It really is an all-day affair, so any time is a good time to swing by Progress Coffee + Beer!

2 IT'S ALL ABOUT CAJUN FOOD AT MUDBUGS

While the name might make you think of this as a dive-y type of place, **MUDBUGS** is anything but! It's actually an upscale restaurant . . . but in a warm and welcoming way. Mudbugs serves elevated Cajun cuisine in a comfortable, family-friendly environment. If you love gumbo, shrimp and grits, and craft cocktails, you're going to love Mudbugs.

Located at the Buda Mill & Grain, Mudbugs has an expansive interior with a long, wooden bar. It's a great spot to stop by for a solo meal, or just pop in for a drink and lunch with a friend. There are also a lot of big tables for groups, both indoors and on the umbrella-shaded outdoor patio.

Mudbugs calls their Cajun food "just shut up and eat it," meaning they're not trying to fit inside a box. You'll see a lot of classic Cajun cuisine on the menu, but there are a few twists and turns, too.

Their crab claws are what dreams are made of. They're served in this luscious bath of butter, white wine,

garlic, and parsley, with plenty of toasted bread on the side for soaking up all that yumminess. And the gumbo at Mudbugs is the best you'll find anywhere! They start with a scratch roux and add plenty of crawfish, andouille sausage, and shrimp. I always crave a bowl of this on a cold day.

The Big Sexy Pasta is exactly that—a big, creamy plate of pasta, confit chicken, Bolognese, and ricotta gnocchi. Yep, it's a lot, but it all pairs together so nicely.

Whether you stay with the familiar po'boys or shrimp 'n' grits with Gouda cream, or you venture to a "Butterboy" 8-ounce filet with blue cheese gratin, topped with truffle oil and lump crab, you're going to be treated well by the friendly staff.

3

STEAK AND SEAFOOD AT TASTE ON MAIN

Like I mentioned before, there's a small historic downtown area in Buda. It's just a few city blocks where locals and visitors can stroll and enjoy shops and restaurants, and it's where you'll find **TASTE ON MAIN**. This is a family-owned steak and seafood restaurant, nestled into a 100-year-old building with exposed brick walls, modern decor, and a large tree-shaded outdoor patio dining space.

Let's start with the cocktails, because they really shine here. Taste on Main has actually become *the* destination for craft cocktails in Buda! You can order from their classic vintage cocktails, or get something original from the Taste specialties. The top shelf margarita rivals the best margaritas in Austin!

The vast food menu has offerings from brunch through lunch and happy hour all the way to dinner, so there are a lot of delicious options here. But I love starting with their five mini ahi tuna tostadas and a half-dozen of the daily oyster offerings. The blackened Texas redfish, creamy seafood linguine, and classic ½ pound smash burger are all popular options for your main entree. But if you're here on a special occasion, ask your server for the butcher block offerings. The most recent time I was there, I splurged on a delicious ribeye paired with a dreamy California Cabernet Sauvignon. I sat outdoors on the patio, listened to the cicadas in the trees, and soaked up the evening air. It was truly the perfect Texas dinner.

4 NIGHTCAPS AND FIRESIDE CHATS AT NATE'S COFFEE & COCKTAILS

Buda residents know that when you need that all-day bar experience where you can meet up with a friend for lattes in the morning or for espresso martinis at 9 p.m., **NATE'S COFFEE & COCKTAILS** is it. This friendly spot at the Buda Mill & Grain development is inside a renovated cotton gin that's more than a century old! The interior has soaring ceilings, a welcoming center bar, and a few TVs scattered throughout for anyone who's hoping to catch the game.

Nate's is a true bar, meaning they focus on drinks and only have a few light bites to accompany the drinks. But you can have food delivered from nearby Buda eateries. (Or just go back through the chapter for a delicious spot for dinner!) The outdoor patio is my favorite place. There's a massive gas fireplace where guests can lounge with their craft cocktail. It's the perfect place to enjoy a drink and a long, slow conversation with a good friend.

THE CRAFT BREWERIES CRAWL

1. **AUSTIN BEER GARDEN BREWING CO.** (ABGB), 1305 W. OLTORF ST., AUSTIN, (512) 298-2242, THEABGB.COM

2. **LAZARUS BREWING CO.**, 1902 E. 6TH ST., AUSTIN, (512) 394-7620, LAZARUSBREWING.COM

3. **LIVE OAK BREWING COMPANY**, 1615 CROZIER LN., DEL VALLE, (512) 385-2299, LIVEOAKBREWING.COM

4. **MEANWHILE BREWING**, 3901 PROMONTORY POINT DR., AUSTIN, (512) 308-3659, MEANWHILEBEER.COM

5. **ST. ELMO BREWING CO.**, 440 E. ST. ELMO RD. G-2, AUSTIN, (737) 300-1965, TOASTTAB.COM

6. **VACANCY BREWING**, 415 E. ST. ELMO RD. 1-D2, (512) 284-9083, VACANCY BREWING.COM

7. **AUSTIN BEERWORKS—SPRINKLE VALLEY**, 10300 SPRINGDALE RD., AUSTIN, (512) 821-2494, AUSTINBEERWORKS.COM

8. **CENTRAL DISTRICT BREWING**, 417 RED RIVER ST., AUSTIN, (512) 993-4511, CENTRALDISTRICTBREWING.COM

9. **HOLD OUT BREWING**, 1208 W. 4TH ST., AUSTIN, (512) 305-3540, HOLDOUT BREWING.COM

10. **ZILKER BREWING CO.**, 1701 E. 6TH ST., AUSTIN, (512) 712-5590, ZILKERBEER.COM

11. **HOPSQUAD BREWING CO.**, 2307 KRAMER LN., AUSTIN, (512) 351-9654, HOPSQUAD.COM

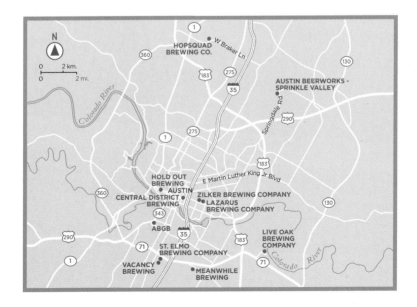

Bonus Crawl!

Craft Breweries

AUSTIN IS A CRAFT BEER DESTINATION. IT IS WIDELY REGARDED as one of the best cities in the United States for craft beer lovers, both in terms of quantity and quality. We just have a ton of breweries, y'all! And they just keep racking up major awards at the World Beer Cup, Great American Beer Festival, and Texas Craft Brewers Cup.

The Austin craft brewery scene is unique in that most of these places are family-friendly. It has actually started to become the expectation for breweries to have places for kids to play, so a lot of these spots have playgrounds, or at least a turf-covered area where kids can kick a soccer ball around. They often have family-friendly food (tacos, pizzas, fries, nachos, whatever), lots of space, and are accommodating to loud 4-year-olds. It's something not every Texas city offers. But for whatever reason, Austin breweries are a family affair.

So, bring the whole crowd to one of these amazing craft breweries in Austin. Order a flight if you want to try a bunch of brews, or just go for a full pint of your favorite. Since a lot of beers in Texas are fairly low ABV (it's HOT here, y'all, and we want light, drinkable lagers!), they're great to sip on while you're enjoying a conversation with friends or watching the kids run around nearby. Cheers!

1

AUSTIN BEER GARDEN BREWING CO. (ABGB)

ABGB specializes in German lagers, which are delicate, crisp beers that taste great by the pint or by the pitcher. Start with a pilsner or helles, which are both always on tap, then move on to try the rotating special beers.

Of course, they didn't earn the "Large Brewpub of the Year" gold medal at Great American Beer Festival three years in a row by serving food that is anything less than exceptional. Big, chewy-crust pizzas are the main food of choice here. A handful of toppings are always available (Margherita, Calabrese, house-made sausage, among others), but the small number of special pies are where ABGB uses fresh, seasonal ingredients to create layers of flavors that will surprise even the most seasoned pizza-eater.

Live music is played on the indoor stage every weekend; if you prefer a quieter dining experience, head outside to rows of picnic tables under twinkly lights. Both choices will give you a perfect Austin evening.

2

LAZARUS BREWING CO.

This is a great brewery in east Austin that, in addition to serving award-winning brews, has some of the best tacos you'll ever try. Even if you're not a really big beer person, use the Mexican street tacos as reason alone to stop by.

But if you do love beer, you're in luck because **LAZARUS** is quite the Austin powerhouse. They're known for the Prodigal Pils, a crisp, German-style pilsner that comes in at 4.8 percent ABV, and their 40 Days and 40 Nights West Coast IPA.

They have a huge patio, and that much space is a rarity in east Austin. It's a great spot to hang out on a Saturday afternoon with a bunch of friends. Grab a beer, a few street tacos, and some of their super thick and crunchy house chips with guacamole, and enjoy all the Austin vibes.

3

LIVE OAK BREWING COMPANY

You've likely seen LIVE OAK Hefeweizen on nearly every tap wall in Austin, but do yourself a favor and head out to Live Oak's brewery in far southeast Austin to try their other European-style lagers, too. This is one of the OG Austin breweries. It started way back in 1997, and since then they've been growing and growing. Now they have a huge property with a modern taproom, a sunken biergarten, and a disc Frisbee course that's a popular place for destination competitions.

Live Oak is kind of a "no nonsense" brewery. They do what they do, and they do it well. If you want a painstakingly crafted Old World–style German lager that rivals the best in the world, this is the place to go.

4

MEANWHILE BREWING

When MEANWHILE announced to Austin that they were building a brand new brewery in southeast Austin, there was a mild amount of buzz about the project. But when it opened, Austin went CRAZY about it! And it's not just because their beer program is incredible and immediately won them some impressive awards, like a Great American Beer Festival medal for their Secret Beach IPA. It's also because the space is so much fun, with a big central tree fort for little ones, multiple award-winning food trucks onsite and a big screen

where they show significant sporting events and movies. There's even a soccer field here!

5

ST. ELMO BREWING CO.

The Yard in south Austin is a really cool mixed-use development area with plenty of fun places to eat and drink, and **ST. ELMO BREWING** was one of the first businesses to establish itself here. Founded in 2016 by two Austin Beerworks alums, St. Elmo is an instantly loveable brewery with a cult-following for its flagship beer, Carl kölsch. In fact, you'll probably see this beer and its recognizable red and white retro logo all over Austin if you're paying attention. St. Elmo has a fun trivia night, a great outdoor patio, and a few excellent food trucks.

6

VACANCY BREWING

VACANCY BREWING is just down the street from St. Elmo Brewing and you could easily knock both of them out in one afternoon of brewery crawling! Brent Watson is responsible for all those delicious lagers, and Sara Hamza is the mastermind behind their beautiful branding. Seriously, this is one of the cutest taprooms in Austin. They won a gold medal at the Great American Beer Festival for their Jet Lag lager, so that's a great place to start on their fairly robust menu.

7 AUSTIN BEERWORKS—SPRINKLE VALLEY

AUSTIN BEERWORKS is one of the OG Austin breweries. This is the beer you'll find on almost every grocery store shelf, bar tap wall, and concert venue concession stand. And it's really solid! These folks care about crafting exceptional beer and building community in Austin. Start with some of their core beers, like Floaty, a session IPA, Pearl Snap, their classic German pilsner, and Peacemaker, their highly drinkable anytime ale.

8 CENTRAL DISTRICT BREWING

Known for their gorgeous downtown Austin taproom and a gold medal at Great American Beer Fest for their Belgian Wit, this brewery isn't the rustic, homemade look that you might expect from a craft brewery. It's a sleek and polished space, made to cater to Austin convention center visitors and downtown Austin residents.

9

HOLD OUT BREWING

Remember Better Half Coffee & Cocktails in the Clarksville chapter? **HOLD OUT** is the craft brewery onsite, which is owned by the same folks but is in its own building. Stop by to visit the brewhouse, the taproom, and the outdoor dining patio. The robust beer list features a wide variety of beer styles, but the hoppy beers are where this Austin craft brewery really shines. Also worth note: The food menu at Hold Out is insane! Try their crispy fried chicken sandwich with a side of curly fries, chana masala Frito pie, or the craveable cobb salad.

What's that? A craveable salad? When it's packed with smoked ham, crispy bacon, big pieces of avocado, and house-made miso ranch dressing, you'd better believe it's something you'll want to order again and again!

10

ZILKER BREWING CO.

Head on over to east Austin to visit **ZILKER BREWING CO.**, a local craft brewery that's small yet mighty. The urban taproom has long picnic tables for family-style seating, a delicious roundup of craft beers, and a brewhouse that's exposed so guests can get a good look at how the beer is made. Spicy Boys, the food truck onsite, has some of the best fried chicken sandwiches in Austin.

11

HOPSQUAD BREWING CO.

If you're heading to watch an Austin FC game at Q2 Stadium, there's no better place to pregame than at HOPSQUAD BREWING. This place is on FIRE on a game day! It's a north Austin Latino-owned brewery with a wide-open industrial taproom, a few food trucks onsite, and a variety of beer styles. Yeah, I realize that sounds a bit vague, but Hopsquad really does brew a pretty big range! I adore their Mexican lager called "El Zapatista" as well as their "Matador" summer ale, but you can find kettle sours, dark beers, European-style lagers, hazy IPAs, and wheat beers. Anything goes, but there's just one rule: If it's game day, make sure you're wearing green. Verde! Listos!

THE BARBECUE CRAWL

1. **FRANKLIN BARBECUE**, 900 E. 11TH ST., AUSTIN, (512) 653-1187, FRANKLINBARBECUE.COM

2. **LA BARBECUE**, 2027 E. CESAR CHAVEZ ST., AUSTIN, (512) 605-9696, LABARBECUE.COM

3. **STILES SWITCH BBQ**, 6610 N. LAMAR BLVD., AUSTIN, (512) 380-9299, STILESSWITCHBBQ.COM

4. **LEROY AND LEWIS BARBECUE**, 5621 EMERALD FOREST DR., AUSTIN, (512) 945-9882, LEROYANDLEWIS.COM

5. **DISTANT RELATIVES**, 3901 PROMONTORY POINT DR., AUSTIN, DISTANTRELATIVESATX.COM

6. **MICKLETHWAIT CRAFT MEATS**, 1309 ROSEWOOD AVE., AUSTIN, (512) 791-5961, CRAFTMEATSAUSTIN.COM

7. **TERRY BLACK'S BARBECUE**, 1003 BARTON SPRINGS RD., AUSTIN, (512) 394-5899, TERRYBLACKSBBQ.COM

8. **BLACK'S BBQ**, 3110 GUADALUPE ST., AUSTIN, (512) 524-0801, BLACKSBBQ.COM

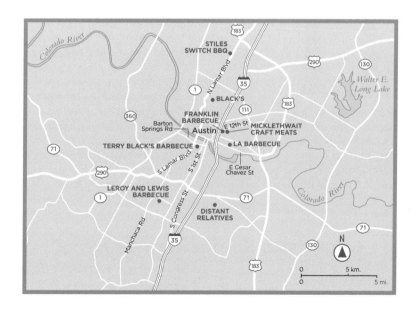

Bonus Crawl!

Barbecue

AUSTIN IS REGARDED AS ONE OF THE BEST BARBECUE CITIES IN the country, so it should be no surprise that I'm including an entire food crawl dedicated to smoked meats. At most of these barbecue joints, the meat is sold by the pound, carved right in front of the customer, and served on butcher paper. Brisket is the star of the show here in Texas, but pork ribs, sausage, turkey, and all sorts of sides are typically available.

As the Austin barbecue scene has evolved, pitmasters have started to get more and more creative with their menus. Gone are the days of typical meat + sides. Now, you find a vegan barbecue fare, a truck that serves barbecue food inspired by the African diaspora, and chefs who care about farm-to-tail and root-to-tip cooking in order to care for the local food scene.

I'm going to walk you through some of the best barbecue spots in Austin, from the internationally renowned giants to the little food trucks you've probably never heard of. Hope you're hungry!

1

FRANKLIN BARBECUE

Behold, the king! **FRANK-LIN BARBECUE**, named after its founder, pitmaster Aaron Franklin, is on everyone's radar, and for good reason. The brisket is melt-in-your-mouth tender, and Franklin Barbecue has won just about every major barbecue award there is, including a James Beard Foundation Award for Best Chef: Southwest and inclusion in *Texas Monthly*'s "50 Best Barbecue Joints in the World."

2

LA BARBECUE

Like most barbecue hotspots, **LA BARBECUE** started as a little food truck. Word started spreading about the ridiculously tasty meat, and lines started forming. Eventually, they outgrew their truck and moved to their beautiful location in east Austin. Lines can be fairly long on the weekends, so stop by on a weekday if you have that option.

3

STILES SWITCH BBQ

This is an old-school Austin barbecue spot, and all of The Who's Who of the barbecue world have probably worked here at one point or another. Since STILES SWITCH is in north Austin and away from the main tourist regions of Austin, the lines aren't as crazy as some of the east Austin barbecue spots (but weekends can get a bit crowded). All of the smoked meat by the pound is fantastic, as is their Buford T's Diablo sandwich: thick piles of brisket, spicy sausage, and jalapeños. Yum!

4

LEROY AND LEWIS BARBECUE

Say hello to the new school barbecue! Evan LeRoy and Sawyer Lewis were tired of every barbecue place serving the exact same menu (brisket, sausage, pork and beef ribs, turkey, sides, and pie), so they decided to open a "new school" barbecue restaurant. The menu rotates, but you can find fun things like beef cheeks, barbacoa-stuffed avocados, and brisket chocolate chip cookies.

> "There's no place in the world that has the concentration of great barbecue that Austin has. The level of competition is high here but that just means more delicious smoked meats for everyone! We're proud to add a unique and elevated take on traditional barbecue as well as support our local farmers and ranchers."
>
> —Evan LeRoy, pitmaster of LeRoy and Lewis Barbecue

This isn't a typical barbecue joint in Austin! James Beard Award semifinalist chef Damien Brockway worked in fine dining before opening this food truck parked at Meanwhile Brewing. The cuisine is modern African American barbecue, showcasing the complicated and complex history of African food in America. Enjoy items like burnt ends with black-eyed peas, pork spare ribs with a super spicy dry rub, and collards in barbecue broth.

6 MICKLETHWAIT CRAFT MEATS

Tom Micklethwait founded his little barbecue trailer in 2012, and it's been recognized in *Texas Monthly*'s "Top 50 Barbecue Joints in Texas" and *Austin Monthly*'s "Best of ATX" multiple times since then. You can find all the regular Texas barbecue meats here, as well as some unique ones like pulled lamb, barbacoa, and special sausage recipes like Thai chile. The sides here are no joke, so be sure to load up on the jalapeño cheese grits, mac-and-cheese, and lemon poppy slaw. This truck is parked at a little beer garden in east Austin, and it's a great hang.

7 TERRY BLACK'S BARBECUE

Twin brothers Mike and Mark Black come from a barbecue family—Black's Barbecue in Lockhart has been open since 1932. After graduating from college and working in the family restaurant (and then just a little bit of a family feud . . .), they decided to open their own smokehouse in the middle of Austin on Barton Springs Road. The long lines wrapping around the building every weekend are a clue into how obsessed Austinites have become with the melt-in-your-mouth brisket, tasty sausage links, and peppery pork ribs.

8 BLACK'S BBQ

Not to be confused with Terry Black's Barbecue, **BLACK'S** is the original barbecue joint that started in Lockhart way back in 1932. They've since opened a few additional locations, and Black's BBQ on Guadalupe is the same slow-smoked meats and delicious classic barbecue sides you can get out in Lockhart.

THE BREAKFAST TACO CRAWL

1. **VERACRUZ ALL NATURAL**, 4208 MANCHACA RD., AUSTIN, VERACRUZALLNATURAL.COM

2. **ONETACO**, 402 BRAZOS ST., AUSTIN, (512) 527-3002, ONETACO.COM

3. **JOE'S BAKERY & COFFEE SHOP**, 2305 E. 7TH ST., AUSTIN, (512) 472-0017, JOESBAKERY.COM

4. **POLVOS**, 2004 S. 1ST ST., AUSTIN, (512) 441-5446, POLVOSAUSTIN.COM

5. **ROSITA'S AL PASTOR**, 1801 E. RIVERSIDE DR., AUSTIN, (512) 442-8402, ROSITASALPASTOR.COM

6. **EL PRIMO**, 2101 S. 1ST ST., AUSTIN, (512) 227-5060, ELPRIMOATX.COM

7. **FRESA'S CHICKEN AL CARBON**, 915 N. LAMAR BLVD., AUSTIN, (512) 428-5077, FRESASCHICKEN.COM

8. **CISCO'S**, 1511 E. 6TH ST., AUSTIN, (512) 478-2420, CISCOSAUSTIN.COM

9. **TACODELI**, 1500 SPYGLASS DR., AUSTIN, (512) 732-0303, TACODELI.COM

10. **TYSON'S TACOS**, 4905 AIRPORT BLVD., AUSTIN, (512) 201-2485, TYSONS TACOS.COM

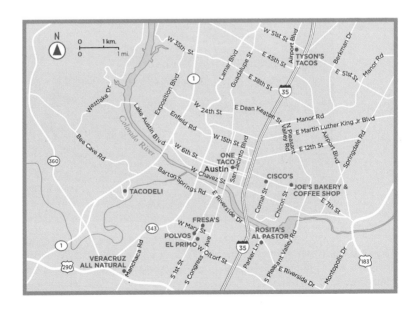

Bonus Crawl!

Breakfast Tacos

BREAKFAST TACOS ARE A RELIGION IN AUSTIN. WALK INTO A coffee shop, and you'll find breakfast tacos more easily than blueberry muffins. What makes a breakfast taco so wonderful? If you're asking that, you clearly haven't tried a great one. Allow me to explain the beauty of a breakfast taco:

They're an entire meal in one hand. Similar to fast-food burgers that are designed to be eaten on the go, breakfast tacos can be consumed while walking with a beverage, like a cup of coffee, in the other hand.

They're inherently delicious. Fluffy tortillas, scrambled eggs, crispy potatoes, salty chorizo, melted cheese, and fresh, homemade salsa. It doesn't take much convincing to get someone excited about these things.

They're simple and cheap. Breakfast tacos aren't overly complicated to make. Anyone can do it. You can make breakfast tacos at home, or you can go out to a taco stand and get a great one for a few bucks.

They can be as healthy or indulgent as you wish. Get a simple breakfast taco with organic scrambled egg whites, black beans, and a few grilled veggies if you're wanting a healthy start to the day, or go to Tyson's and get the B is for Bacon (double bacon, potato, egg, and cheese) if you're vacationing and just want to live a little.

Read on to explore some of the best breakfast tacos in Austin, from the old classics to the new chains, the best taco trucks, and some fun new fusion tacos.

1 VERACRUZ ALL NATURAL

You might have read about Veracruz All Natural in the Downtown Austin chapter, but it's worth repeating: These tacos are amazing! Their migas taco is widely regarded as the best breakfast taco in Austin. After the Food Network recognized their tacos as among the top five in the nation, word spread pretty quickly and **VERACRUZ ALL NATURAL** was able to open multiple trailers and a couple brick and mortars around Austin. My favorite location is the walk-up window next to the Congress Avenue bridge. I love to enjoy a morning walk by the lake and then get a breakfast taco to enjoy afterward.

2 ONETACO

These insanely tasty breakfast tacos already had a huge fan base even before they were featured on *Diners, Drive-ins and Dives*. They're simply delicious! With multiple locations around Austin, it's easy to get your "I Heart Bacon" breakfast taco, or the unique pancake taco (yes, it's a breakfast taco served in a pancake instead of a flour tortilla!) whenever the craving hits.

3 JOE'S BAKERY & COFFEE SHOP

JOE'S BAKERY has been a family-run staple in Austin since 1962. They make their own tortillas, pastries, and big, hearty breakfast plates. The breakfast tacos run for just a couple dollars each, and one or two tacos should fill up the average breakfast eater. Their *carne guisada* is hearty and cozy on a cold morning, and the bacon and egg is a customer favorite on any day of the week. Locals and visitors love this place; expect crowds!

4 POLVOS

While there are many excellent breakfast taco fillings in Austin, there are surprisingly few places that make their own homemade flour tortillas, and **POLVOS** is one of them. My favorite time of day to stop in for a Polvos breakfast taco is right when they open. There's a cook standing in the corner, flipping fresh, hot tortillas and grilling tomatoes for the homemade salsa bar. These are massive breakfast tacos with pick-your-own fillings. Try the egg-bacon-cheese or egg-bean-potato for starters.

5

ROSITA'S AL PASTOR

If you're on the hunt for a hole-in-the-wall spot with legitimate Tex-Mex cuisine, you have to try **ROSITA'S AL PAS-TOR**. It's been open since 1985, and they serve customers from a food truck, but this is where you'll find some of the best breakfast tacos in Austin. Fresh, homemade tortillas, still dusted in flour, are filled with the yummiest flavors. Don't skimp on the homemade salsa!

6

EL PRIMO

If you're eager to check off a food truck and a breakfast taco in the same morning, stop by **EL PRIMO** for some tasty tacos at this little Mexican food truck. Go basic with the chorizo, egg, and cheese, or get some delicious barbacoa or *lengua* if you're feeling a bit more adventurous.

7 FRESA'S CHICKEN AL CARBON

FRESA'S has already been mentioned in the Bouldin Creek chapter, but it's worth mentioning to remind you that their breakfast tacos are incredible. They're served on homemade flour tortillas and full of scrumptious fillings like steak and eggs, big slices of avocado, and homemade pico de gallo. They have a few locations in Austin, but the South First Street location has a walk-up window, perfect for mornings when you need a quick and satisfying breakfast on the go.

8 CISCO'S

This classic Austin bakery is named after Rudy "Cisco" Cisneros, and they've been making breakfast tacos, big plates of Mexican food, and homemade biscuits since 1950 in their iconic blue building on East 6th Street. Plenty of famous Austin politicians have eaten here; you'll see pictures of Lyndon Johnson and Bob Bullock plastered to the walls in the back room. The breakfast tacos are big and filling; start with the migas taco or a sausage/egg.

9 TACODELI

If you want to start a heated debate with a group of Austinites, ask them which Austin-based taco chain makes better breakfast tacos: Torchy's (South Congress crawl), or **TACODELI**. Torchy's is by far the larger chain, with locations outside of Texas, but Tacodeli has an extremely loyal fan base, locally sourced ingredients, and new locations in big Texas cities like Houston and Dallas. Their breakfast tacos are available at any of the Austin locations, and they're also delivered to dozens of coffee shops around Austin. You won't

have to look very hard to find them. The Otto is a crowd-pleaser with organic refried beans, double bacon, avocado, and jack cheese, and the Jess Special is a typical migas taco with loads of avocado added on top. Or just skip the menu entirely and create your own with two, three, or even four ingredients nestled inside a fresh tortilla. Top it off with their famous creamy jalapeño Doña salsa.

10 TYSON'S TACOS

If the crowd of people doesn't lure you in, the smell might. **TYSON'S TACOS** has their own smoker in the back, and the air is full of delicious smoky flavor. If you're looking for the best breakfast tacos in Austin, try their Avocado *Abogado*. It's a big flour tortilla full of egg, ribeye, avocado, and skillet potatoes. And if you're craving a lunch or dinner taco,

try to get the Burnt Ends taco before it sells out. It is, as described, filled with burnt ends, onion rings, pickled jalapeños, and Valentina cream. If you have any hunger left at all, enjoy working your way through this endless taco menu. And if you've reached your limit, no worries! They're open 24 hours, so you can come back whenever the taco craving strikes.

Appendix

Eateries by Cuisine and Specialty

American
Better Half Coffee & Cocktails, 118
Birdie's, 108
DrinkWell, 168
Geraldine's, 20
Josephine House, 116
Launderette, 86
Lenoir, 66
Mattie's at Green Pastures, 56
Olamaie, 138
Summer House on Music Lane, 42
Taste on Main, 230
T22 Chicken Joint, 196

Argentinian
Bueno Aires Café, 104

Asian
Bar Peached, 126
Chi'Lantro BBQ, 74
Komé, 164
Lin Asian Bar + Dim Sum, 124
Lucky Robot, 44
Peached Tortilla, The, 186
Qi Modern Chinese, 12
Ramen Tatsu-Ya, 75
Thai Fresh, 62

Bakery
Brentwood Social House, 184
Quack's 43rd Street Bakery, 148
Sugar Mama's Bakeshop, 58
Upper Crust Bakery, 174

Bar
Crown & Anchor Pub, 140
De Nada Cantina, 88
DrinkWell, 168
Golden Rule, 222
Half Step, 26
Holiday on 7th, 90
Lustre Pearl, 30

Small Victory, 14
Watertrade, 50
Workhorse Bar, 171
Yard Bar, 199

Barbecue
Black's BBQ, 247
Distant Relatives, 246
Franklin Barbecue, 244
La Barbecue, 244
LeRoy and Lewis Barbecue, 245
Loro Asian Smokehouse, 76
Micklethwait Craft Meats, 246
Stiles Switch BBQ, 245
Terry Black's Barbecue, 247

Beer
Austin Beer Garden Brewing Co.,
   236
Austin Beerworks—Sprinkle Valley,
   239
Banger's Sausage House and Beer
   Garden, 22
Central District Brewing, 239
Hold Out Brewing, 240
Hopsquad Brewing Co., 241
Lazarus Brewing Company, 236
Live Oak Brewing Company, 237
Meanwhile Brewing, 237
Pinthouse Pizza, 182
St. Elmo Brewing Co., 238
Vacancy Brewing, 238
Zilker Brewing Co., 240

Breakfast
Bird Bird Biscuit, 178
Bouldin Creek Cafe, 54
Juiceland, 146
Monument Café, 219
Nervous Charlie's, 176
Sweet Lemon Kitchen, 210
Walton's Fancy and Staple, 9
Patika, 72

Acknowledgments

There's no Austin Food Crawls without a bunch of fantastic Austin restaurants, and there are no restaurants without the humans who decided to create them. So . . .

To the Austin chefs and restaurant owners: You are incredible. You work so hard and are so underappreciated. Thank you for caring not just about the quality of the food that you serve, but where it comes from and how that impacts our earth. Your restaurants are where we go to celebrate life's greatest events, process the hard stuff, welcome guests in town, go on first dates, enjoy the warm Austin evenings, or just sit and drink a beer after an exhausting day at work. Austin isn't Austin without you, and what you're doing really matters.

To my kind and patient husband, Nate: Thanks for a million things, but for the purpose of this book, thanks for being the most supportive as I constantly had to duck out to visit "just one more restaurant!" Thanks for challenging me to slow down and be curious.

To my beautiful boys, Milo and Dayton: You're my favorite little Austin companions! You two make pretty much everything more fun. Thanks for keeping me laughing and helping me to constantly see the world through a different perspective. Also, here's a secret I'm willing to share: I love it when your grimy little toddler fingers sneak into the corners of my photos.

And finally, to my big extended family and all the ways you continue to support my hobby-turned-side-hustle-turned-business. Gathering around lots of good food and wine has always been our family's thing. I know that my desire to write a food book is rooted in some of my earliest memories of dining out with my grandparents, Bob and Mary Fran, who helped me discover the joy of a really great restaurant. I love you all.

Index

About the Author

KELSEY KENNEDY writes to more than a quarter of a million monthly readers in her popular Austin restaurant and lifestyle blog *So Much Life*, as well as her three Texas travel blogs: *The Austin Things*, *The San Antonio Things*, and *The Waco Things*. Her approachable and uplifting writing style paired with her specific interest in the independent restaurant scene of Austin has quickly made her the go-to for both visitors and local Austinites on where to eat next. Her blogs have been featured in *Austin Monthly*, *Eater Austin*, and *Austin Woman*.

Kelsey lives in south Austin with her husband, Nate, and her two sons, Milo and Dayton.